WHAT MAKES US

Southern

Fifteen enduring symbols of the South reveal much about our character, and encourage us to slow our stride.

Our State

DOWN HOME IN NORTH CAROLINA

WHAT MAKES US

Southern

Published by *Our State* magazine, Greensboro, N.C.

What Makes Us Southern
copyright © 2013 by *Our State* magazine.
All rights reserved.
Published by Mann Media Inc.
P.O. Box 4552, Greensboro, N.C. 27404
(800) 948-1409 | ourstate.com
Printed in the United States by R.R. Donnelley

editor ELIZABETH HUDSON

designer JASON CHENIER

illustrator JOSEPH EDWARDS

Library of Congress Control Number: 2013905902

WHAT MAKES US

Southern

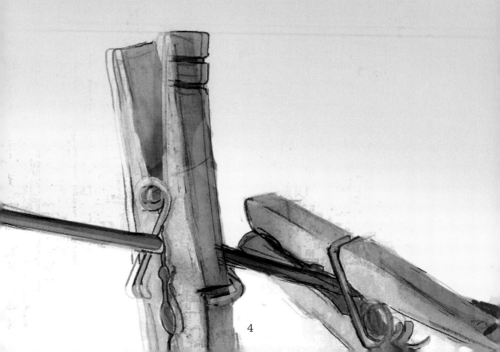

TABLE OF CONTENTS

Southern HOSPITALITY

by SCOTT HULER

In the South, we welcome you.
We welcome you to sit at our supper tables,
stay at our bed and breakfasts, sleep late
in our famous hotels. And we'll give you
a smile as big as you've ever seen.
Thank you for your kindness.

A SINGLE FACT RENDERS POINTLESS all debate about whether to live north or south of the Mason-Dixon Line. You can talk about college basketball or NASCAR or barbecue or grits until the metaphorical cows come home — you'll alienate as many people as you convince, I'm sure of it. Those are all topics that prompt debate, that profit from debate. But when I moved to North Carolina from, well, somewhere else, within a week I realized I had come home. My awakening involved soda pop.

In a cozy booth with coworkers, I decided to give myself the treat of a second Diet Pepsi as I lingered over lunch with newfound friends. The waitress refilled my glass and did an amazing thing — she did not pick up the bill and scrawl in another drink, the way waitresses in, well, other places did to my lunch checks for a decade. I thought I'd found a special restaurant I'd return to for years. That happened to be true, but by the end of the first week of those welcome-to-town lunches, I realized something: That's just how it works here in the South. You get as many sodas —

or iced teas — as you want with lunch. You can get involved in a good conversation, decide the heck with work, and sit there until 3 p.m. And the drinks just keep coming.

To me, that tastes a lot like heaven.

Of course, I soon realized: That's not heaven; it's just the perfect expression of Southern hospitality. The endless soda pop refill is "Go on, set a spell" made flesh. The free refill says, "You had enough, Sug? You sure? Lemme just get you a little more. Stick around. Don't hurry off. Be comfortable. Stay."

But hospitality has another side, of course, and soon after I moved to the South — 20 years ago, mind you — I experienced that, too. I went to dinner at a nationally known Durham restaurant one evening and emerged four hours later, glassy eyed, with the Northern members of my party delighted: "Now that," they said, "was Southern hospitality."

"No," I said. "That was a hostage drama." That wasn't "Welcome." That was, "Stick around whether you like it or not; you are going to sit there and claw your way through our food performance and our three different dessert services, and we'll tell you when you're full." That wasn't hospitality —

that was showing off. It was manipulation served on a bed of grits. "Oh, no, folks, you ain't done yet," that restaurant said. "Stay."

STAY: THAT ULTIMATE expression of hospitality, somewhere between request and command, not only the urge to a beloved guest, but also the rebuke to a misbehaving child or dog. In the lunch booth, with the free soda pop and the ceiling fans and the chummy waitress, Southern hos-

> ## "Graciousness is both armor and a weapon."

pitality is all it's chalked up to be: It's 12-molar, 190-proof distilled essence of welcome, and aren't you sweet? But at the restaurant where you can't leave until they bring you a bill, and they won't bring it until they're good and done with you, it's about control, not welcome. It's a little bit more like Grandma's insistence on red velvet cake and seven-layer cake and chocolate cake after Sunday dinner — but everybody has to make one and bring it, and don't even think about getting up from the table until you've tried all three, and, meanwhile, greens turn to glop on the stove and dressing dries out in the oven and Grandma accidentally lays the potatoes down on the settee, a case of nerves brought on by the strain of all these guests that she demanded come over. I have endured this kind of hospitality in the family of my beloved wife, a native of this state, and I have seen the toll it takes on host and guest alike. "A tyrannical Southern insistence on hospitality" is how David Denby described it in a recent *New Yorker* review. "Graciousness," he concluded, "is both armor and a weapon."

Denby is far from the first to note that Southern hospitality has its dark side. Roy Blount Jr. discussed it in his famous essay "The Lowdown on Southern Hospitality." "The truth is, irritation is involved in Southern hospitality," Blount writes. "Nothing ... is sweeter than mounting irritation prolongedly held close to the bosom."

Good point, but I have to ask: That applies to all hospitality, does it not? I grew up in Ohio, and although I welcome guests and love to share bed, board, and company, I'm usually tired of the visitors almost from the moment they take off their coats. In any case, I'm internally rehearsing my many sacrifices on their behalf and looking forward to when they leave. I think that irritation attends all hospitality, and it

highlights the complexity of the human condition rather than anything particularly Southern.

Not so the free soda pop — that is definitely a Southern thing. Seriously — I return to this time after time because it has real meaning to me. I have encouraged people to move to North Carolina for the free soda pop alone. I have grown so familiar with the free refills at some of my favorite haunts that I have been welcomed to go behind the bar and get it myself, like a houseguest finally, after a prolonged stay, no longer waited on but given free rein to the fridge and cupboards. Now that is hospitality.

I came to the South as a journalist, so from the start, I was showing up on people's porches and doorsteps, imposing on their hospitality, and let me say straightforwardly: That hospitality never failed. I would ask shocking questions about their organ transplants and their murdered children, their strange customs and their perplexing works of art. They would share their stories with me, and we would laugh together, cry together, eat together. Remember this, I would say to myself. This is where you live. This is how people do here.

So, OK, there's something to this hospitality business. But from where? And since when? If you go to the books — I always go to the books —

you quickly learn that like many things perceived as stereotypically Southern, hospitality has a flavor more rural than simply Southern. That is, the roots of this famous hospitality probably stem from the fact that the South, unlike the citified North, was a community of mostly farms, large and small.

In *A History of the South*, Francis Butler Simkins and Charles Pierce Roland say "the cult of Southern hospitality" expressed "a means of relieving the loneliness of those living far from each other." A new friend once pressed hospitality on me on Malta, the island at the belly button of the Mediterranean. When I suggested I could not possibly be as welcome a guest as he made me seem, he explained: "We live on an island. We wait for people like you." Loneliness powerfully motivates hospitality. On a more basic level, when it took half a day to get to the neighbors, you'd better get more than a ladle of water and a nod from the porch when you rode up.

On the other hand, Frederick Law Olmsted, who traveled throughout the South before the Civil War and wrote of his experiences, expected to pay 75 cents or more each night for the hospitality he received. Hospitality had become a myth even before then. Jacob Abbott's 1835 *New England, and Her Institutions* describes a traveler riding "through Virginia or Carolina" who is all but kidnapped for no other reason than for the householder he visits to shower him with hospitality. Abbott claims that such hospitality explains why the taverns of the South were so poor: "so they must continue, as long as Southerners are as free, and generous, and open-hearted as they now are." Apocryphal stories abounded of plantation owners who had slaves waylay strangers into their clutches, the better to demonstrate hospitality. The slaves, meanwhile, presumably knew what it felt like to be required to stay rather longer than they might have wished.

The competitive hospitality macho of, say, the Twelve Oaks barbecue in *Gone with the Wind* is long gone, and with it the perceived need to try to dress up the overzealous hospitality of slavery. The "cult of hospitality," however, remains. In 1972, Simkins and Roland explained that in the Old South "the forests, the fields, and the streams gave abundantly of their produce," and even a small Southern farm encouraged hospitality by providing its owner with "nearly all the vegetables known to the American housekeeper of the twentieth century." In some ways that seems to predict the modern Southern gardener creeping to the neighbor's door in dark of night to "hospitably" abandon a bushel of excess zucchini.

Still, it seems unlikely that farmers were inveigling unwary passersby to their overburdened groaning boards just to avoid throwing away good food.

WHATEVER ITS ORIGINS and however extreme its exaggerations, only a fool would claim that hospitality has vanished from the modern South. If you think I was thrilled when I first discovered the Miracle of the Endless Soda Pop, I only wish you could have seen me at my first NASCAR race, wandering the infield at Charlotte Motor Speedway from grill to grill, from cooler to cooler, getting fuller and more hospitable with every step. One almost had to duck to avoid the constantly proffered beer, burger, or barbecue. And if the cries at bikini-clad women in the infield strained propriety, nobody who has walked the infield trails can deny that in the face of such rudeness many a young woman has been moved nonetheless to show her … hospitality.

An even greater modern expression of Southern hospitality comes at the end of a pickup tailgate in the parking lot around, say, Carter-Finley Stadium in Raleigh any time after 10 a.m. on a home Saturday in the fall (although the stadium could just as easily be Dowdy-Ficklen in Greenville, or Kidd Brewer in Boone; this tradition spreads over the state like red clay runoff from a construction site). In these pregame parking rituals, that antebellum competitive hospitality has returned: Graciousness, Denby said, is both armor and weapon. The clang of battle rings, with SUVs rocking cookware that would make the chef at that restaurant that once held me hostage weep with envy.

Yes, graciousness is armor and weapon. But it's also, simply, gracious. Southern hospitality may have started because Southerners were a rural people, and it may have codified into a fierce code and a laughable myth — how many steps from Scarlett to Clampett? It may cover our greatest sins and enable our most manipulative behaviors. But it also lets us, as a group, agree on something. Down here, in the South, we're nice to each other. We share; we've got enough. Stick around and enjoy a little more. Don't hurry off. Sure, you're a Yankee, but here you are, and here we are, and have a little more soda pop. Be with us — be one of us. Be comfortable.

We're glad you're here.

Stay.

Tomato
SANDWICH

by SCOTT HULER

The classic tomato sandwich's roots may reach beyond the Mason-Dixon line, but there's something about this summer staple that gives it a special home in our kitchens.

WHAT I AM GOING TO SAY may cause some discomfort. But I urge you to hear me out, for in the end I bring a message of joy.

I hope you won't begrudge my first premise, which is that Southerners, proud of a regional culture with roots as deep as the red clay, have something of a propensity to claim things. It's hard to deny this, right? Whether it's porches or storytelling, acoustic music or the land itself, Southerners take pride in not only their traditions, but also the contributions of those traditions to the culture at large — and can even, on occasion, stretch those contributions a tad. For example, I'm almost sure there are writers outside the South, although once your region has produced William Faulkner and Eudora Welty, Harper Lee and Lee Smith, you can be forgiven for being a bit self-congratulatory.

Southerners can be especially proprietary about food. Whether it's grits or okra or collard greens or anything else on an almost numberless list, Southerners say it belongs, somehow, exclusively to the South. Which makes it perhaps all the more an affront that I must, after thoroughly researching the topic, make the following statement: The tomato sandwich is not a Southern food.

Yes, I know: the tomato sandwich. Two pieces of white bread: Merita, say, or Wonder; maybe Bunny, if you're from Tennessee. Duke's mayonnaise — and only Duke's mayonnaise, about which more later. A thick slice of tomato, dripping oozy goodness. A little salt and pepper, if you like.

WHATEVER I'M SAYING is that it's not a Southern thing at all, that tomato sandwich. As my own community-supported agriculture farmer Tom Kumpf says, "That's not a Southern classic. That's a *summer* classic." Kumpf grows tomatoes on his Double T Farm in Garner, south of Raleigh. In fact, the tomato is why Kumpf's farm exists. "What really got me go-

ing in the garden was wanting to eat my own tomatoes," he says. And who can blame him? A fresh-picked tomato, still radiating the sunshine that grew it? That's heaven on earth.

"Because if it's not dripping down your chin while you're eating it over the sink, it doesn't count."

CRAIG LEHOULLIER IS a Raleigh tomato maven whose website, NCTomatoman.com, casts a long shadow on the North Carolina heirloom tomato landscape. Among his accomplishments is the popularization of the sandwich-friendly 'Cherokee purple' tomato, famed for the nice meatiness that holds a tomato sandwich together. He lived all over the country, and he prefers his tomatoes in slices on grilled-cheese sandwiches.

Whatever else goes on a sandwich, LeHoullier says, "the tomato is critical." As an heirloom tomato guy, he strongly believes a good sandwich needs an heirloom tomato. "You go to the farmers market," he says, of hybrid tomatoes, "and you see piles of the big, red, perfectly round ones. If you tossed them at someone with any kind of speed, you'd probably injure them for life." The favorite heirlooms of the Carolinas, both Kumpf and LeHoullier say, are the 'Cherokee purple' and especially the 'German Johnson', a North Carolina native cultivar that's a great big beefsteak, which basically means it slices well.

LeHoullier also has no loyalty to the store-bought white bread of the classic sandwich, preferring a nice ciabatta or farm bread. And then he utters the greatest apostasy of all. "I don't eat mayonnaise," he says. "I've probably never eaten what is called the great Southern tomato sandwich."

That sandwich, if it exists, has Duke's mayonnaise on it. "On both sides," says Erin Corning, Duke's associate brand manager. "Because if it's not dripping down your chin while you're eating it over the sink, it doesn't count."

The tomato sandwich is Duke's signature recipe, "the quintessential meal that Duke's graces," Corning says — above all, because "it doesn't require a whole lot of instruction." Bread, tomato, mayonnaise. And she can (and does) go into significant detail about mayonnaise ingredients. Duke's gets its tartness by using no sugar, for example. Kumpf and LeHoullier, too, talk for hours about things like the balance of acid and sweet in a tomato, explaining the difference between a red and a pink, bringing up names that expose the fancies dreamed up for paint colors as the frauds they are. You might imagine painting your bedroom 'salmon mousse' or 'Savannah clay,' but a tomato variety named 'Eva Purple Ball'? Or, my favorite, 'Debbie' (it's a red-orange beefsteak)? Now that's putting a name on something.

BUT AS FOR INGREDIENTS, if you're looking past tomato, mayonnaise, bread, you're overthinking the tomato sandwich. For even there, as good as Duke's mayonnaise is, I am not prepared to yield that a local type of mayonnaise stakes an entire sandwich to a region, or that putting a piece of mozzarella or some basil on it renders it somehow inauthentic. I watched my mother make her tomato sandwiches with Miracle Whip (she tells me she's switched to Hellmann's now) in northeastern Ohio; you make them with Duke's on your Carolina front porch. How does that make the tomato sandwich a Southern food? It's like the South claiming bread, or the clothesline, or elbows. True, where would we be without them, but it seems to me the Union soldiers probably appreciated them as much as the boys in gray.

And if my own mother is not proof enough, the library gives you unimpeachable evidence of the cosmopolitan nature of the tomato sandwich. No less a literary personage than Harriet the Spy took a tomato sandwich to school every day for five years — "her mouth watered at the memory of the mayonnaise," Louise Fitzhugh tells us. And Harriet, mind you, lived on the upper East Side. That's not even the south of Manhattan.

Speaking of my mother, by the way, and where I watched her slap the Miracle Whip on the tomato sandwiches of my youth — you will already have discerned that I am Not From Around Here. But I beg you — do not allow that fact to cause you to dismiss my inquiries. If you prick me, I may not bleed vinegar-based barbecue sauce, but I have lived in North Carolina since 1992. I have two native Tar Heel children. I married a native Tar Heel girl. I have strong opinions on NASCAR racing (pro), grits (con), and ACC basketball rivalries (let's just not start). I know I'll never be a true Southerner, but I've been here two decades, and I mean to stay.

Much like the tomato itself. Leaving out the trumped-up controversy over whether it's a fruit or a vegetable (biologically, it's obviously a fruit; linguistically it's both, depending on when and how you eat it — on a tomato sandwich, it's a vegetable), the tomato has

the proud history of any immigrant. It originated in South America, then made its way north through Native American routes as far as Mexico, where the Aztec cultivated it, calling it "xitomatl." Its passage to the American South took it through Europe, after Cortes brought some back from Mexico. Europeans called it "golden apple," because the first ones they saw were gold. The Europeans cultivated them starting in the 1540s, and the first reference to them in the New World came in 1710, when William Salmon published an English guide describing tomatoes he had seen in Carolina. From there, it spread throughout the country. Tales of terror about tomatoes as poisonous plants are mostly that — tall tales; American cookbooks and almanacs as early as the mid-1700s describe managing and consuming tomatoes.

SO MY POINT COULD NOT be more thoroughly made: The tomato sandwich is a summer, not a Southern, food. It belongs to the world, not the South. If Southerners think it's theirs, they are wrong. My conclusion is simple, well supported, and straightforward.

So, of course, cue backpedaling.

Once I had drawn my conclusions, I did what I usually do and sat down to discuss them with my wife, June Spence. Raleigh native, lover of food and all good things, June spoke about tomatoes and tomato sandwiches in a way that was, for lack of a better word, Southern.

She gave the same recipe as everyone else: Duke's mayonnaise, a thick slice of tomato, and white bread, although she admitted that she uses whole wheat nowadays. And June herself questioned the sandwich's status: "I don't think it's Southern," she says. Anyhow, less Southern than rural: "It's just what you get when you've got a lot of people growing tomatoes in their gardens."

Like in ... the South?

"It's because you're growing plenty, you've got a bunch of them," she says. "One thing we always had in the summer as a side dish was sliced up tomatoes with salt and pepper on them. It was just the abundance." In a place like the South, where the growing season starts earlier and lasts longer.

"My grandmother just had rows and rows of them," June went on. Her grandmother lived in the tiny Harnett County town of Angier. "As soon as they were ripe and as long as the plants lasted, there would always be a windowsill-full. And you'd always get sent home with them."

So, a homegrown crop with a long growing season, consumed constantly by people used to doing for themselves, and a sandwich that's a quick and con-venient way to eat it. With a native condiment that somehow makes it special. Maybe the tomato sandwich, Southern style, does have a claim to iconic status. In fact, maybe that tomato sandwich and I have a few things in common. Like me, the tomato showed up here in the South as an immigrant — and stayed. In fact, it's gone all over the world, but somehow it seems to have found a special place for itself here, prospered, and made a home.

Which describes the modern South right down to the kudzu, yes? A place of simple things with long stories, where immigrants bring new ingredients and make them work, changing them but leaving them still somehow themselves, perhaps even more themselves for the newness. Grandma, after all, rarely made shrimp and grits, but nobody says grits are ruined now.

So maybe we can say about the tomato sandwich that it started off rural and made its way into the cities, started out Southern and made its way elsewhere, started out classic and absorbed change, from white bread to wheat, from Duke's to Miracle Whip to Hellmann's. It started out simple and grew complex.

Or maybe we say this: The tomato sandwich is as Southern as ... as Southern as ... as Southern as anything else.

RED *Clay*

by CHIP WOMICK

In central North Carolina, red clay is the sod beneath our feet, the bed from which nourishment springs, a source of work and of art. And for those of us whose roots are planted here, it colors who we are.

I NEVER SAW RED CLAY growing up in southeastern North Carolina. Robeson County soil is sandy, not like the beaches where we vacationed every summer, but a far cry from dense red clay.

I was about 10 or 11, when I visited a family who lived on a farm — relatives, I think, although I can't recall for sure who they were or where they lived. But it was the first time red mud clung like glue to the soles of my shoes.

What I remember vividly is that it had rained, and the downpour had pooled in bare places between the farmhouse and the barn and the fields and the pigsty. They didn't have grass in the yard like we did in town. Their "yard" was red muck. Someone had laid boards here and there and scattered straw in a few places to make walking easier. I'd never seen the like. They didn't seem to notice.

From that weekend until I moved to Randolph County in my early 20s, I equated red mud with farms, slogging through mire to slop hogs and leaving shoes at the back door so you wouldn't track red footprints on the floor.

RED CLAY, WHICH OWES its hue to iron, left an imprint in my mind. But it didn't permeate my being, not like I figure it colored the lives of the farm family I visited. And not like it helped shape the life of my current neighbor, a fellow named John Brooks.

didn't get covered in dust when it was dry or red soup when it was wet. And when the chores were done, he and his brothers and other boys would strike up a game of baseball in a field.

"We called it cow pasture ball, running through cow turds and all that," he says. "Back then, you didn't have no amusement. You had to make your own amusement. It was some tough sleddin' in those days, I swear it was."

Later, he would take his skills to honest-to-goodness baseball diamonds in towns across the state, with green grass and dirt base paths of red or yellow or brown. His talents on the

"We stayed in the dirt about all the time."

When Brooks was a boy in rural Randolph County, red clay touched him at almost every turn. "We stayed in the dirt about all the time," he says.

He helped his daddy plow red clay fields to plant the cotton and soybeans and such that sustained them. He walked to school along the unpaved road that sliced between forest and fields in the countryside between the mill communities of Ramseur and Coleridge, sticking to the edges so he

field landed him a job in a textile mill. He was hired to operate a machine that knit ladies' hose during the days, and to pitch for the factory team on the side, challenging other mill teams for league bragging rights.

But before that, Brooks's daddy died. John was just 14, the second oldest of six children. He wanted to stay in school. But working on the farm and their small dairy, milking a handful of cows by hand, left little time for tending to studies. He dropped out in the 10th grade to go to work so he could feed his mama and five brothers and sisters.

They raised almost everything they needed to survive.

"We didn't know hardly what money was," he says. "You better believe you had a job all the time. 'Bout every young'un had certain chores they had to do to keep things going."

When the dirt soiled their clothes, they had no fancy automatic machines to wash them. John's mama boiled meat scraps and lye until the "juice" was gone. When the mixture cooled, she cut it, like biscuits, into cakes of soap. Then the work began. "You had to scrub the clothes on a dadburn scrub board," he says.

Eventually, his mama sold the family farm, and Brooks left the farming life behind. But he's always had a garden at his home — and often an even larger plot somewhere out in the country — for a couple of reasons: Fresh food is better than store-bought; and it's in his blood.

But this year, he didn't plant a garden on the slope of reddish clay that is his backyard in Ramseur, a place where he's grown corn and beans and tomatoes and more for at least 35 years. It's not because he's tired of urging seeds to sprout and sprouts to grow from a spectrum of clay. It's because his knees are worn out after 90 years of walking — and working — this red land.

BY SUMMER'S END, knee-high weeds most likely will overrun his garden spot. Red clay, he says, grows good weeds.

If Brooks is a measuring stick, red clay grows good people, too. Like Brooks, generations of other good, hard-working inhabitants of central North Carolina have reckoned with the red land. What doesn't kill us makes us stronger, or so the saying goes. It might also make us smarter — or more creative. A handful of industrious souls found a different way to master red clay: Potters shape it to their will.

Venture into the working sheds out behind Owens Pottery on Busbee Road in rural Moore County, where the floors are dirt and everything is decorated with dust, and you'll see how it was done. Here, the business of making pottery is accomplished the old-fashioned way, says Boyd Owens. His grandfather, James H. Owen (Owen's son, M.L., apparently added the "s" to the family name), established the operation on this spot in 1895, making it the oldest pottery shop in the Tar Heel state.

Most modern-day potters buy their clay in bags of powder, like large sacks of flour, and they mix it with water to make their working clay. Boyd and some of his kin at nearby Jugtown Pottery don't do it that way. A couple or three times a year, they travel to secret spots to dig tons of red clay out of the ground, from about two feet beneath the topsoil, and haul it home. Some of the clay is dug within 10 miles of the pottery shop. They harvest it in Randolph, Moore, and Lee counties; they know of a sweet spot of clay down in South Carolina. Boyd Owens's daddy, M.L. Owens, located most of those clay caches.

"My daddy went out prospecting for clay all the time. If he was out on the road, he was probably out looking for clay. Basically, we still use the clays he found." M.L. also developed, circa 1945, a signature red Owens glaze. The red clay makes the red glaze redder. "There's something about that red body of clay that gives it depth," he says. "We like for it to have a deep scarlet look to it."

To prepare the native red soil for turning on a potter's wheel, it's spread for drying in piles a few inches thick, then, weeks, maybe months, later, it's run through a hammermill, an hours-long job that slowly pulverizes the clay. An engine on an old Super C Farmall tractor powers the hammer-

mill. They've tried rigging up other motors, but "dust gets the best of the engines," Owens says.

The powder is mixed in a pug mill, which produces thick, bologna-sized sticks of clay. After it's processed in a de-airing machine, it's ready for the potter's wheel. "It's usually a pretty good turning clay," Owens says, "and probably not as refined as what you'd buy from a company."

That's why, he says, most potters purchase powdered clay. They can count on store-bought clay being consistent. There's another thing: Doing it the old-fashioned way is work.

"It's truly a dirty, physical job, messing with clay," Owens says. "But at the end of the day, it's a pretty good, feel-good job."

DOWN THE ROAD A SHORT WAYS from Owens Pottery, you'll find Westmoore Pottery, where the husband-and-wife team of David and Mary Farrell have been working for more than 30 years. Their focus is producing wares with the look and feel of pottery from the 17th, 18th, and 19th centuries — plates and cups and bowls and muffin pans and more that are made to be used. They have supplied replica pottery for such period films as *Amistad* and *Cold Mountain*.

Before 1800, Mary Farrell says, almost all of the pottery produced in the area was made from red clay. It was available and quick: "They'd just use clay dug from the ground, and that was it." Consequently, she says, you can find rocks bulging from the sides of some pottery.

"I think one reason I like the red clay is that in the past so many things were made out of it."

The Farrells combine five powdered clays to make their signature redware.

"I think one reason I like the red clay," she says, "is that in the past so many things were made out of it. It's a little bit finicky, particularly if you don't use any lead, [and] it's kind of hard to find a glaze that works."

They also have a clay pit nearby. David and one of their sons chiseled the hole in the ground a shovelful at a time. The lad was not taken with pot-making, but he loved to dig. For his part, David made red clay tiles and fired them in a kiln. He's replacing the wooden shingles on the pottery shop with the red rectangles. Along the roof ridge, he laid red pottery jugs sliced in half lengthwise. He expects the tiles to last as long as the shop and jokingly says he hopes the framework will support the weight. Really, he's confident that it will: He made it, too.

Mary Farrell says visitors to Westmoore Pottery occasionally ask what they use to make the pottery. When told that it is clay, some reply that it looks like dirt. Well, it is dirt.

"You don't even think of it as clay or dirt," she says, "even though it is dirt. If you're gardening, you have more of a sense of, gosh, I'm really dirty. When you get your hands in it [on the wheel], you don't think that you're sticking your hands in dirt. You're thinking more about what it's going to become."

What is the red clay going to become?

That, of course, depends on whose hands are tilling it — or turning it — and how hard those hands work.

Clotheslines

by ROBERT LONG

Hanging clothes is more than pinning garments on a line. It tells you something about your neighbors, and it tells them something about you. For one of the state's most beloved artistic families, hanging clothes brings them closer to home.

THROUGH MY EARLY CHILD-HOOD the washer was a necessity and the dryer was a luxury — every family had a clothesline. I still remember ours. The line in the back of our house stretched from the crab apple tree to the pecan tree in the middle of the yard. We had a long, forked, wooden pole that we used to support the middle of the line when laundry hung from it. As kids, we ducked under the line when we ran through the yard or played catch.

This clothesline stayed in place until 1989, when Hurricane Hugo blew down the pecan tree along with a dozen or so other trees in our yard. When my schoolteacher parents, William Ivey Long Sr. and Mary Wood Long, took our family to our house in Manteo, one of my first chores was to take the coil of slightly mildewed clothesline rope from the screened porch and tie it in between the pine trees in the backyard. That clothesline saw a lot of action. To this day, leaving the pins on the line seems almost naughty.

I remember our clothesline in the backyard of the campus house that we shared with another faculty family when I was in elementary school. Our family lived upstairs and the Scott family lived downstairs with their four children. Somehow, we all shared the clothesline in the backyard. As kids, we used the clothesline for badminton or volleyball nets and, best of all, to hold sheets and bedspreads that our mothers let us use to create puppet theaters and other stages. That backyard was pretty magical for a 6-year-old, and the clothesline was the best part.

In spite of my early affinities with our backyard lines, the clothesline was a thing of the past for me as soon as I left home for college. The neighborhood Laundromat became my laundry of choice for the next 20 years, followed by the washer and dryer in the basement of my first home. I thought of the clothesline as a relic of my childhood to which I would never need or want to return.

IN THE 1950s, clothes dryers and air conditioners drove us inside our homes, leaving backyard clotheslines and front porches as reminders of a time long gone. Before that, the clothesline provided quiet opportunities for an older generation to pass something to the next generation.

A generation ago, the backyard clothesline prompted conversations between neighbors.

My children didn't learn much from watching me stuff the wet laundry into the dryer. I began to see how modern conveniences could take away: As the clothes dryer evolved from a luxury to a necessity in American culture, a valued part of everyday life was left behind.

A generation ago, the backyard clothesline prompted conversations between neighbors. People shared recipes, discussed homemade remedies. The garments hung on a clothesline and how they were hung told neighbors the size, age, adult occupation, economic status, and tidiness of the new family that moved in.

Years later, my simple clothesline pulled me out of the house where I could experience nature and the seasons, where I could wave to neighbors, where I could see for myself what weather might lie ahead for the upcoming day.

MY WIFE, ANNE, AND I blended our families a dozen years ago, and we began preparing clean laundry for seven young children. I took the role of collecting, washing, drying, folding, and distributing the laundry, while Anne handled the more thoughtful and demanding work. About eight years ago, I needed to figure out a way to keep our new dog, Rosie, an energetic Border collie-and-spaniel mix, from following the kids to school. I found a 50-foot-long dog run at the hardware store and strung it between the side of the house and a poplar. The run consisted of a length of plastic-covered wire, with a shorter wire hanging from a pulley that rode up and down the run, allowing Rosie to run back and forth in either direction. Rosie and the dog run didn't get along, and Rosie won. On an early spring day, I thought our newly washed socks and underwear might dry faster in the dryer if they didn't have to compete with the blue jeans and sweatshirts. I scrounged up some

clothespins and took a heavy basket of wet jeans, towels, and T-shirts out the side door. Without much thought, I hung the load of laundry on Rosie's old dog run.

Over the next few months, I began to use the line about once a week. Each time I took a basket of wet laundry outside, I thought, "But it's easier to use the dryer." Sometimes the clothes got wet from a rain shower. Occasionally, I forgot to bring the clothes in until after dark, and I held a small flashlight in my mouth while I unpinned the clothes dampened with dew.

Still, I kept my clothesline "thing" under wraps. I saw each new basket of laundry as an organizational challenge. I concocted theories about how to hang the individual pieces to create the best opportunity to dry. Pants and shirts dried best if hung upside down. I looked for ways to hang the wet clothes more quickly, using fewer clothespins. My clothesline work began to resemble a time-and-motion study.

My quest was good for a couple of months. I knew it was time to seek some advice from Anne; I summoned up my courage and confessed. I expected her to laugh, but she didn't. "I know," she said, "and it is so good for the children to see you doing this. After all, we're modeling our behavior and showing them the value of household work."

Now, I had an audience.

Color became as important as clothing type in the sequence of hanging. I experimented with color sequences, as well as with the size and shape of the article. I concocted my own Code of Clothesline Ethics — I would not manipulate the contents of the laundry basket for my own creations. I would accept whatever came out of the wash. I began my quest to discover the air-drying technique that would keep the kids from complaining about scratchy towels, which to this day I am still trying to perfect.

A year into my clothesline quest, I carried the laundry basket outside and reached down to grab the first piece. I brought up a red T-shirt and hung it on the line. Not knowing exactly what my artistic point of view was that morning, I pulled up a lighter piece of clothing, followed by a pair of orange shorts. Keeping in mind my basic knowledge of color theory from a high school art class, I picked out a yellow T-shirt. I began to feel a trickle of apprehension. ROY G. BIV. Red, orange, yellow, green, blue, indigo, and violet — the colors of the rainbow.

There was no stopping me now.

Folk history suggests that sailors invented the clothesline; they had rope, knew how to tie knots, and didn't have a convenient riverside bush or boulder on which to dry their clothes. They also had time to whittle the first clothespins, to pass the time during the doldrums.

But no one knows who really created the first clothesline.

Laundry dries in the dryer for the same reason that laundry dries on the clothesline: evaporation. Wet fabric dries as the water molecules turn into vapor and leave the fabric. Heat and motion assist with the evaporation. This is why laundry dries faster on the line when it is sunny and breezy, and when the humidity is low. Laundry might not dry if it is sunny and breezy with 100 percent humidity; there is nowhere for the water molecules to go. Laundry will dry when it is freezing and especially if there is a breeze, as long as the humidity is low.

Even in the winter of 2011 — one of the coldest winters on record — our clothes dried on the line.

Laundry on the clothesline will dry almost anywhere, given a chance.

SEVERAL YEARS PASSED before I told friends that I was using the clothesline, and when I did, I spoke of it as a joke. But my friends didn't laugh. They, too, appreciated the clothesline.

My friend Neil lives down the road in the old Mill House. He's lived here nearly 40 years since he moved to North Carolina to study philosophy at Duke University. When Neil was growing up in Buffalo, New York, a woman down the street hung her sheets out in the fresh air in the wintertime. Of course, they were frozen stiff as plywood.

"In the afternoon, she would march out to the backyard, give them some karate chops, and angle them in the door to take to the basement to let them thaw out," he says. "She never used the dryer for sheets."

In North Carolina, Neil discovered he could hang clothes on the line year-round. He hangs clothes at 11 a.m. in the winter and gathers them at 4 p.m. "Hanging clothes outside to dry is close to a religious experience for me, peaceful and meditative," he says. "No mechanical dryer could come close to giving me the satisfaction I get from my clothesline."

Clotheslines had a profound effect on my brother, William. We grew up surrounded by fabric — costumes, old clothes, uniforms — and you must clean that fabric. Irene Rains, the former costumer for the Carolina Playmakers in Chapel Hill and the annual production of *The Lost Colony* on Roanoke Island, taught William more about the care of fabric than anyone. For more than 25 years, Irene was responsible for the creation and care of hundreds of costumes that actors wore nightly.

"Every dry and sunny day during the summer, her costume crew would string hundreds of feet of temporary clotheslines zigzagging across the backstage area of the Waterside Theatre," he told me. "It was here that I first experienced the true art and beauty of clothes, and in this case costumes, being hung on lines to dry and to soak in the freshness of the summer breeze and the purifying sunlight."

LAST OCTOBER, ANNE AND I visited our daughter Anna in Asheville. We met Anna at her house on South Grove Street, a few blocks from downtown. After a tour of her house, Anna told us she had something important for us to see. As she opened the door to her back deck, she pointed to her new clothesline, which was strung between the house and a tree. On the line was a load of laundry. My mind fast-forwarded through images of my mother hanging clothes on the line, images of our bathing suits fresh from the beach dripping in the backyard, images of backyard puppet theaters, and my memory of Anne's advice about setting examples for our kids. As I looked out over Anna's backyard, I knew I had passed this on to the next generation.

Barbecue

by JIMMY TOMLIN

The battle for superior pork — chopped or sliced, vinegar or tomato, whole-hog or shoulder — depends on which side of the barbecue-fixins' line you're on.

FOURSCORE AND 7 BILLION hush puppies ago, our North Carolina forefathers drew the battle lines for a war that rages still today — the clash for barbecue supremacy in the Old North State. Historians who are paid to know such things tell us the barbecue battle has been a heated conflict marked by decades of inflammatory words, but which, as far as we know, fortunately has never actually escalated to bloodshed.

Unless, of course, you count the hogs. Untold millions of porkers have become casualties in this epic struggle for barbecue bragging rights in the Tar Heel State — but no humans. This is, after all, a civil war.

The apparent Mason-Dixon line — which is marked off in hush puppy crumbs and will heretofore be referred to as the barbecue-fixin's line — slices vertically through the state somewhere around Raleigh, dividing the land into two distinct, uncompromising, unapologetic schools of thought about the hallowed preparation of barbecue and its mandatory side dishes. And therein lies the root of the conflict.

ing for the honor of eastern-style barbecue are veterans such as Wilber's Barbecue in Goldsboro and the Skylight Inn in Ayden; carrying the battle flag for western-style barbecue are traditional strongholds such as Lexington's own Lexington Barbecue and Stamey's Old-Fashioned

Squaring off in the culinary war are eastern-style barbecue and Lexington-style barbecue.

IN NORTH CAROLINA, barbecue is a sacred cow — I mean, um, sacred pig. We learn to eat it a certain way — determined, of course, by which side of the barbecue-fixin's line we live on — and our reverence for that style of barbecue is almost spiritual. Poke fun at our particular pork preference, and, well, them's fightin' words.

Squaring off in the culinary war are eastern-style barbecue, the barbecue of choice east of the barbecue-fixin's line (including Raleigh), and Lexington-style barbecue, which originated in Lexington and has been more or less adopted by barbecue joints west of the barbecue-fixin's line. Fight-

Barbecue in Greensboro.

While several factors contribute to the escalating conflict between east and west, one of the most significant points of contention is a difference of opinion about which parts of the pig should be included when cooking the barbecue. Down east, for example, barbecue chefs go whole hog — literally — as their barbecue includes meat from the shoulders, hams, and loin. Lexington-style barbecue, on the other hand, is strictly pork shoulders. Proponents from both sides argue passionately that their particular style — and no other style — is barbecue as God intended it to be.

"YOU MIGHT THINK, 'Well who would know the difference?' But it does make a difference," says barbecue historian and connoisseur Bob Garner of Burlington, author of *North Carolina Barbecue: Flavored By Time*.

"The shoulders are a darker meat with more fat," Garner explains. "Eastern style adds meat from the hams and loin, which is lighter. It's also leaner, so eastern barbecue tends to be a little bit drier." The other major difference between the two styles lies in the barbecue sauce. Down east, the meat is seasoned with a concoction similar to a popular table condiment used in Colonial days — a blend of vinegar, red and black pepper, salt, and maybe a swig of oyster juice — to help mask the gamey taste of various meats, according to Garner. Lexington-style barbecue features a sweeter, redder sauce that consists of the same vinegar base, but which has been sweetened with white or brown sugar and also contains tomatoes.

What often happens during wars is that the people doing the fighting get so caught up in the heat of the battle that they tend to lose sight of how and why the war even began in the first place, and that appears to be the case with North Carolina's barbecue civil war, too.

It seems that a couple of newspaper journalists — Jerry Bledsoe, formerly of the old *Greensboro Daily News*, and Dennis Rogers of the *Raleigh News & Observer* — fanned the flames of war through their respective columns, in which each man spewed tongue-in-cheek observations about the other's beloved style of barbecue.

In *North Carolina Barbecue: Flavored by Time*, Garner cites an exchange between the two writers: "In the East," Bledsoe wrote, "you get all these little things in your mouth and wonder what the hell they are. They're ground-up skin. That's the only way they have to give the meat any flavor. So what you're getting is roast pork and ground skin with a little vinegar and hot peppers and salt on it."

Rogers countered by poking fun at the Lexington-style custom of offering sliced barbecue, which you would never find down east: "When I am hankering for a big piece of dead hog meat with tomato sauce, I like to follow the advice of my good friend Jerry Bledsoe and head west, where you find lots of it. For some silly reason, Jerry calls that barbecue."

Somewhere along the way, North Carolinians became fiercely loyal to the barbecue style served in their region of the state. "For a long time, all they knew about the other style of barbecue was what they had heard," Garner says. "A lot of people in the eastern part of the state would swear they served a thick, ketchup-based sauce in the west, because they didn't know any better. They'd say, 'I hate that stuff.' 'Have you ever tried it?' 'Well, no.'" But even among those who have sampled both, Garner says, "most people tend to think the best barbecue is whatever they got used to when they were growing up."

FOR THE SAKE OF ACCURACY, there are other differences between the two styles of barbecue in North Carolina. For example, wood-smoked meat is more prevalent in the Piedmont, whereas barbecue chefs down east cook mostly with gas or electricity. Brunswick stew is a common side dish down east, but the Lexington-style restaurants add French fries instead. (Hush puppies, by the way, are a universal side dish.)

And then there's the matter of another side dish, the slaw. In the eastern part of the state, barbecue is served with a white or yellow slaw; in the Piedmont, you get red slaw. But near the middle of the state, there's a curious phenomenon that Garner refers to as "barbecue schizophrenia."

> **In the eastern part of the state, barbecue is served with a white or yellow slaw; in the Piedmont, you get red slaw.**

"There is sort of a no-man's land around Burlington and Mebane," Garner says. "where you'll find quite a few places that can't decide whether to serve white or red slaw, so they actually serve pink slaw."

Whether these slaw splitters are sympathizers or — even worse — traitors is not clear. What is clear, however, is that if some other state attacks our barbecue culture, we will call a cease-fire, circle the wagons, and defend our sacred honor. We may differ as to whether eastern-style or Lexington-style barbecue is best, but when it comes to national reputation, we all agree that North Carolina-style is best. On some matters, there's simply no need to fight.

TEN TO TRY

1 Allen & Son Barbecue
6203 Millhouse Road
Chapel Hill, N.C. 27516
(919) 942-7576
Lunch and dinner, Tuesday-Saturday

2 B's Barbecue
751 B's Barbecue Road
Greenville, N.C. 27834
Lunch, Tuesday-Saturday
until the barbecue runs out

3 Bridges Barbecue Lodge
2000 East Dixon Boulevard
Shelby, N.C. 28152
(704) 482-8567
Lunch and dinner,
Wednesday-Sunday

4 Lexington Barbecue
10 U.S. Highway 29/70 South
Lexington, N.C. 27295
(336) 249-9814
Lunch and dinner, Monday-Saturday

5 Little Richard's Lexington BBQ
4885 Country Club Road
Winston-Salem, N.C. 27104
(336) 760-3457
Lunch and dinner, Monday-Saturday
Second location: 5353 Gumtree Road,
Wallburg, N.C. 27373
(336) 769-4227

6 The Pit Authentic Barbecue
328 West Davie Street
Raleigh, N.C. 27601
(919) 890-4500
Lunch and dinner daily

7 Short Sugars Pit Bar-B-Q
1328 South Scales Street
Reidsville, N.C. 27320
(336) 342-7487
Breakfast, lunch, and dinner,
Monday-Saturday

8 The Skylight Inn
4617 South Lee Street
Ayden, N.C. 28513
(252) 746-4113
Lunch and dinner, Monday-Saturday

9 Stamey's Old Fashioned Barbecue
2206 High Point Road
Greensboro, N.C. 27403
(336) 299-9888
Lunch and dinner, Monday-Saturday
Second location: 2812 Battleground
Avenue, Greensboro, N.C. 27408
(336) 288-9275

10 Wilber's Barbecue
4172 U.S. Highway 70 East
Goldsboro, N.C. 27534
(919) 778-5218
Breakfast, lunch, and dinner, daily

LONGLEAF
Pine

by JIM DODSON

For centuries, the pines have
towered over the Sandhills.
They anchored our state's nascent
economy and, to this day, harbor life.

ON A DEWY SUNDAY morning not long ago, I took our dogs, Mulligan and Ella, to meet the world's oldest longleaf pine. It sits in a forest no more than half a mile from our home in Southern Pines.

To get there required a short hike through the lush grounds of Weymouth Center for the Arts, the former ancestral home of celebrated Algonquin Round Table novelist (and Scott Fitzgerald cohort) James Boyd and his wife, Katharine. We followed a series of sandy bridle paths through a forest of majestic pines, one of the few remaining stands of old-growth longleaf pines on the planet, surviving elders of a vast forest of the legendary tree that once covered an estimated 90 million acres of southeastern America. Today, the domain of the mighty longleaf — memorialized in a famous toast, lynchpin of the Old North State's first economy — has dwindled to less than two million acres.

I knew right where to find this particular patriarch because I'd recently attended its special "birthday party," put on by the state-owned Weymouth Woods-Sandhills Nature Preserve. Out of simple curiosity, I'd joined 50 or so of my neighbors who turned out to hear a ranger lecture on the struggle to save the endangered longleaf and one of the most unique ecosystems on earth.

"Well, here it is," I announced to the girls with a sweaty flourish as we reached the base of the famous tree, a mighty longleaf that was roughly five feet in circumference and rose maybe 130 feet into the air, ending in a green canopy of gnarled limbs and distinctive, elongated needles. "The oldest living longleaf on earth."

TRUTHFULLY, THE GIRLS DIDN'T appear terribly impressed by either the big tree or my little speech, even after I carefully pointed out that it was standing there at least 200 years before America organized itself as a nation and probably germinated about the time the paint was still drying on Leonardo's Mona Lisa.

Ella, the golden retriever, plopped down, panting, and gazed up the tree's trunk with what might have been construed as mild interest, although I suspect she was simply glad to catch a breather and was mostly interested in the honeybees. For her part, Mulligan, a young flat-haired retriever who spent her early days foraging for food in the longleaf forests of southern Moore County before I found her trotting along on a lonesome highway, scanned the surrounding terrain for any sign of wildlife. Once a hunter, always a hunter, is her motto.

In fairness to the girls, or for that matter many residents of Southern Pines and neighboring Pinehurst, we live in the midst of an old and stunning longleaf forest that is fairly easy to take for granted. If you've seen one ancient longleaf pine, one could easily argue, you've pretty much seen them all — tall, stately, with a crown of beautiful, long needles that seem to inevitably wind up underfoot wherever you go. The towns and villages of the Carolina Sandhills are covered in longleaf pine trees.

But as I learned from the ranger's birthday talk, if we appreciated how vital this mythic native pine and its prodigious ancestors were to the economic and social development of the state and the high quality of life we enjoy now, *Pinus palustris* might not be in the trouble it's in today, down 97 percent from an original native range that stretched from Tidewater Virginia to eastern Texas.

THE FIRST COLONISTS USED the slow-growing pine to make their stockade settlements and shipped the tall, strong timbers home to Britain to be used as ship masts. The greatest threat, however, arrived in the mid-19th century, when production of tar, pitch, and turpentine — prized by the shipbuilding trade of several nations for waterproofing planks and rigging on ships to make them impervious to sea and salt-air corrosion — reached its peak of production. Ironically, the state's first true export industry also managed to turn vast acres of longleaf forests into desolate, sandy wastelands vulnerable to wildfire and erosion.

Apart from the abundant wildlife that typically inhabits a mature longleaf forest — more than 100 species of birds, reptiles, insects, foxes, bobcats, and the forest's unique brawny fox squirrel that feeds directly off the calorie-laden longleaf pinecone — the symbiotic struggle for life is best symbolized by the majestic Red-cockaded Woodpecker, which prefers to make its nesting cavity in the wood of living longleafs. As the domain of the mighty longleaf declined, the indigenous woodpecker became endangered along with its host tree.

LIKE MANY CAROLINIANS, my first introduction to this veritable Eden in the Pines occurred when my dad brought me down the road from Greensboro as a golf-mad teenager in the late 1960s to experience the splendors of America's first golfing resort, Pinehurst. I understood even then that, apart from the legends who made pilgrimages here to the lush fairways of the self-styled "Home of American Golf," there was something wholly unique about this pine-girdled arboretum.

In truth, it took me many years before I learned that it was the effect of these unique pine trees — and not, as commonly believed, golf — that created the world-renowned Village of Pinehurst. Half-a-dozen years before Boston soda fountain magnate James Walker Tufts hired Donald Ross to begin laying out his first golf course, Tufts was lured to the region by reports of the remarkable healing properties ascribed to the longleaf pine.

The idealized New England village Tufts created was initially designed to cure the respiratory ailments of all classes of congested travelers from the North and Midwest. Something about the dry, fragrant, pine-scented air, he and many others believed, worked magic on ailing lungs. The lore and image of the longleaf pine figured prominently in early marketing of the resort and at least a dozen other early hotels of the region, all of which incorporated the winsome "pine" theme into their names for obvious reasons.

The dry, fragrant, pine-scented air worked magic.

SEVERAL YEARS AGO, while researching the life of reclusive golf star Ben Hogan, I sat with my good friend John Derr on the porch of beloved Pine Crest Inn discussing Hogan's stunning breakthrough at Pinehurst's celebrated North and South Championship in the spring of 1940. Before his arrival in The Pines, as locals call the area, Hogan had notched several second-place finishes but failed to win his first tournament. Within days of winning the North and South, however, he went on a tear that resulted in subsequent victories at Greensboro and Asheville — one of the game's most scintillating debuts ever.

"Ben told me that if he hadn't won at Pinehurst, he might well have quit the Tour," explained Derr, who followed Hogan every step of the way as a young reporter for the *Greensboro Daily News* before heading off to serve in the United States Army and then to an illustrious broadcasting career for CBS Sports. "But he always maintained that this place cured him and sent him down the road to stardom."

"What cured him?" I asked the ageless Derr, who was then approaching 90.

He gave me a roguish grin. "That's part of the mystery and allure of this place, exactly why old man Tufts came here. I personally think it had something to do with the pine trees, the peaceful air of the longleaf. There is something magical about them, you know."

NOT LONG AFTER THE GIRLS and I hiked through the forest to pay respects to the world's oldest surviving longleaf, I met Derr again for one of our semi-regular chats on the Pine Crest porch — in this instance to also congratulate him on being named to the Order of the Longleaf Pine, the highest honor that can be bestowed upon a citizen of the Old North State. Notable recipients include The Rev. Billy Graham, poet Maya Angelou, artist Bob Timberlake, and Derr's old CBS colleague, Charles Kuralt.

I asked Derr how he felt about this rare honor, given its association with the state's legendary pine tree. "Oh, it's a tremendous thrill," declared the Gastonia native. "You know, they only give it to you when you reach the age of a mature longleaf pine. And they grow to be very old indeed."

John is in his mid-90s now, but I decided not to tell him what the girls and I had recently learned — mid-90s would barely make him a longleaf teenager. Instead, I lofted my glass to honor him — and the mythic pine of our home state.

"Here's to you and the land of the longleaf pine," I said, taking a stab at quoting the opening stanza of the whimsical verse Leonara Martin and Mary Burke Kerr wrote in 1904, a ditty the North Carolina General Assembly adopted as the state's official state toast in 1957.

Derr, ever the showman, grinned and finished the stanza in his finest broadcaster's voice.

"*... The summer land where the sun doth shine / Where the weak grow strong and the strong grow great / Here's to 'Down Home,' the 'Old North State.'* "

And with that, we drank to the longleaf's continued good health, not to mention our own.

SWEET

Tea

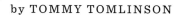

by TOMMY TOMLINSON

In our dining rooms and diners, we stir together a handful of humble ingredients to produce an amber elixir that tastes like the South and feels like home.

"OK, THIS IS HOW WE MAKE the sweet tea," Anita Hall says. Anita has waited tables for at least 25 years here at Pressley Park, a meat-and-three a few miles south of uptown Charlotte. She shows up at 3:45 a.m. to brew tea for the cops and construction workers who want breakfast before dawn, and the families who take home jugs for the weekend, and the guy from Baltimore who picks up two gallons every time he goes home so he has something to drink with his crab cakes. This tea is the color of a base-ball glove, but clear enough to see through. And in one cold glass you taste the South — the sweetness of a hunk of cane sugar, the tannins of a black-water creek.

The joke at Pressley Park is that Anita doesn't drink the tea — she likes coffee better. But every morning she starts making tea, and by closing time at 3 p.m., they'll have gone through 35 to 40 gallons.

it out, but they aren't about to give the secret up.

The truth is that there's a secret something in every glass of good sweet tea. You can doll it up if you have a mind to, but all you really need are tea bags and sugar and water.

Somehow, though, when you put them together, it's magic.

And over the years, in this part of the world, sweet tea has become infused with meaning. It's more than just a drink.

"So you take this" — a five-gallon container — "and put the tea in and fill it halfway with hot water," Anita says. "Then stir in the sugar. Then put in more water. Then we put in a little …"

And all of a sudden, three voices holler, "No!"

One belongs to George Gregory, who runs Pressley Park. The others belong to his dad and mom, Andy and Tina, who opened the restaurant and still help out. It turns out there's a secret something in the sweet tea. They'll laugh when you try to figure

PEOPLE DIVIDE THE SOUTH from the North at the Mason-Dixon Line, but I've always thought the real marker is the sweet-tea line — the point where, at the next diner north, they don't have sweet tea ready to pour. I'm not sure just where the line is. I feel sorry for those poor souls up above it. But one thing's for sure: North Carolina is on the good side.

And over the years, in this part of the world, sweet tea has become infused with meaning. It's more than just a drink.

Sweet tea is our alchemy — our gift of making something special from humble ingredients. (Just like barbecue, conjured into glory from the cheapest cuts of meat.) Sweet tea is our love offering, poured for family and neighbors and even the guy trying to sell us new gutters. And at its most basic, sweet tea is a cold blast on a hot day, like a dip in a river from the inside out.

We have been drinking sweet tea down here for nearly two centuries now, although the tea of the early 1800s doesn't much resemble what most of us drink with cornbread and greens. Back then, the tea was green tea, and it was served as an ingredient in punch — spiked with champagne or rum, and sweetened with sugar and cream.

By the early 20th century, most people in the South drank black tea imported from China or India. (All types of tea come from the same species of tea plant, *Camellia sinensis*; the different types of tea come from different varieties or how the leaves are processed.) Cookbooks had recipes for basic sweet tea, but people still drank it mostly in punches. The two big events that converted the South to the sweet tea we know today were Prohibition, which got rid of (most of) the nation's alcohol, and ice delivery, which gave people a way to cool down a big glass. By the 1930s, sweet iced tea was as common at the Carolina table as salt and pepper shakers.

YOU CAN BUY SWEET TEA all over the country now, way past the sweet-tea line. McDonald's sells it nationwide. Just about any convenience store sells a bottled or canned version; you can even find it in vending machines. But if you're in North Carolina, and you buy sweet tea in a can … well, bless your heart. Maybe you could just hide it in a paper bag. What we're talking about, when we talk about sweet tea, is something brewed that morning, stirred by hand, served by a waitress who calls you darlin', poured out of one of those special pitchers with the spout on the side, or better yet, sitting in the fridge at your mama's house.

Deet Gilbert teaches about tea as part of her Essentials of Dining Services class at Johnson & Wales University in Charlotte. Part of her job is to help future restaurant managers understand the economics of tea — it's so cheap to make that sometimes the ice in the glass costs more. (Even with free refills, tea is one of the biggest profit-makers on the menu.) But she also wants her students to understand the culture of tea, all over the world, and especially in the South.

"Those tea punches, back in the 1800s, were made for social events," she says. "And I think that tradition has continued, even though tea has also become something you'd just normally have at the table. A glass of tea is the first thing you bring out when you have a guest in the house. It's the connection you make with someone to make them feel welcome."

Even within the simple sweet-tea trinity — tea bags, sugar, water — there are all kinds of variations. Some people steep the tea for half an hour, some let it sit all day. Some people throw in a couple extra bags to boost the astringency — the thing that makes your mouth a little dry, like a glass of red wine. And then there's the sugar. "I know some places you feel like you better have a good dentist before you drink the tea," Gilbert says.

That's true — every so often, you'll take a swig of tea that would be better off poured over pancakes.

Sweet tea is homemade. And it's part of how you make your home.

But this is part of what makes sweet tea so intoxicating. It's homemade, if by "home" you mean all those little Formica diners and smoke-smudged barbecue joints scattered across North Carolina like pepper flakes. One day, the tea guy's not paying attention and dumps in too much sugar. Or your sister's making it at home and ends up one bag short. Or you're off up North somewhere, trying to turn Lipton's finest and tap water from a glacier lake into something that reminds you of a summer night in Wilkesboro.

Sweet tea is homemade. And it's part of how you make your home.

ANDY AND TINA GREGORY, the folks at Pressley Park, put a lot of work into their sweet tea. They arrived in Charlotte 30-some years ago from Greece, after a brief stop in Boston. When they opened their first restaurant, the House of Pizza, they didn't know how to make sweet tea. But every day they brewed a pot, and every day they asked their customers how it could be better. After a few weeks, nobody complained anymore.

They say they haven't changed the formula since — and that goes for the secret ingredient, too. It's great sweet tea. But the truth is, it tastes a little different every day — depending on how hot the water is, and how many strokes Anita Hall takes when she stirs the sugar in, and what time of day you order it. There's no magic formula, because sweet tea is about people. That's the magic part.

FRONT Porches

by TIM BASS

Even when the space is still there —
a front porch with room for a couple of
rockers, maybe a swing — time to enjoy
the tranquility seems to have moved
just beyond our grasp.

IN MY MIND, I CAN SEE THEM. They slip in from the past. It's early evening, near dark, and the whole family has drifted out of the house and settled in seats on the front porch. The father rubs his round belly. The mother wields a fly swatter. Three of the children jam into the swing, while the littlest ones climb onto laps. A dog thumps its tail on the floor. In the closing hours of the day, the family will take in the night air and let supper settle. They will talk some, perhaps sing or tell tales, and they'll catch up on the latest with any neighbors who happen by.

Let your imagination wander back several decades — to the 1930s, say, or the '20s, or earlier — and you'll see them, too: the whole crowd, all of them collected on the front porch to while away the time before sleep. Same as last night. Same as tomorrow night. They have no television and likely no radio. Certainly no Internet, no portable electronics. To get what passes for entertainment, they have that covered stretch between the house and the yard, a place not in and not out, somewhere to go without having to go anywhere.

We can see them, but only from a vague distance. Most of the porch people have left us. And I wonder: Did they take simpler times with them? Did they carry away the notion of filling the day's slow hours by simply sitting and letting the world breathe?

"YOU HAVE TO KIND OF LIVE IT," says Chuck Pennington, co-owner of The Verandas bed and breakfast in Wilmington's Historic District. The 8,500-square-foot Italianate house has the perfect front porch — a high, wide expanse equipped with wicker chairs behind a white-picket railing. The place invites guests to return to those long-ago nights of porch life.

"It's just a total life-enriching kind of experience," Pennington says. "You sit and stop. You don't have the BlackBerry. You don't have 30 million emails. It's a quality of life that people have lost."

He's right. People stay indoors now, near walls of wired components and flashing blue screens. These days, we escape by looking in, not out.

Except for a few souls who haven't given up on the front porch.

There's this old man I see when I ride my bicycle out on the coastal roads of Carteret County. He sits in a little chair beside the storm door of a small, white house along N.C. Highway 12 on Cedar Island. Over the years, we've kind of gotten to know each other — or at least I think he recognizes me as I pedal by, tired and sweaty. He waves, and so do I. I shout a greeting, and I hear his in return. He keeps sitting, and I keep riding.

Of course, the old man might not distinguish me from anybody else. Maybe he's the most neighborly man on the outer reaches of Carteret County, the grand greeter of Cedar Island, and he occupies his front-porch throne and raises a friendly hand toward everybody, foreign or familiar, on two wheels or four.

Then there is Shawn Johnson,

a 17-year-old who spends time on the front porch of his aunt's house on Wooster Street in Wilmington. I found him out there one day, sitting

"We've been so occupied with technology and stuff. I think we need to have some outside time, to get away from some things.

alone, sunk into a patio chair. He held a cell phone, which he didn't check — no calls, no text messages. He had his feet reared high on the metal railing, the toes of his sneakers poking over the edge.

"I'd rather be outside to feel the air and see people, see how things have changed," he said, sounding like the youngest old man I'd ever met. "We've been so occupied with technology and stuff. I think we need to have some outside time, to get away from some things. You can be more in tune with a conversation outside than you can inside."

The house once belonged to Shawn's grandmother, who is gone now. Shawn remembers all the time she spent on her porch, watching traffic roll toward the Cape Fear River and visiting with anyone who came along on foot. Shawn has made that his way, too.

"Sometimes, you've got to get out and talk to somebody, look around," he said. "It kind of relieves your stress, lets you think about things. I guess you could think in the house. I'd rather think outside."

SHAWN WOULD FIT RIGHT IN with my parents. They live in Clinton, the seat of Sampson County, and after supper they often take to the green rocking chairs on their front porch. From there, they survey the low-key scene: a neighbor mows the lawn, another neighbor walks a dog, still another cruises past on the way to who knows where. Over there, a man pulls weeds on his surgically repaired knees. Here comes a man moving with the aid of a walker, then a mother and daughter lost in conversation, then a woman striding a power pace.

My parents watch the routine from their perch on the porch. They say hey to everybody within earshot, and those who pass say hey back. (In

51

Clinton, no one says "hello" unless they're answering a telephone.) Folks drift away from the street and up to the porch to trade news: who's sick and who's on the mend, who's got a new baby and who's got a new car, and it'll soon be time for collards. Everybody agrees: We sure could use a good rain.

This is old-style social networking, a throwback to the pre-computer age, when families made a habit out of doing nothing special. They just sat on the porch and greeted folks one passerby at a time. These days, that's pretty special.

the last time he came home.

MY OWN FRONT PORCH is just a stoop, a puny concrete pad rimmed with bricks. It makes my house look less like a box, but the porch is too small, not as big as a minute. If I put a rocking chair out there, I'd tumble onto the lawn.

Clearly, the contractor who built the houses on my street carried no

And there they would sit, the whole bunch rowed up on the porch, everyone lazy and immobile.

WE HAVE A PICTURE of my older brother on that porch. Somebody snapped it years ago, when he took a trip up from Florida to visit my parents. We forgot about the photo until March of this year, when we found it in his briefcase, three days after he died of a heart attack that came without a hint of warning. In the picture, Nick sits in one of the green rockers while wearing a baseball cap and shorts. He gives the lens his self-satisfied grin. He appears happy. It was

nostalgia for those long-ago Carolina nights when families waddled away from their supper tables and headed for the front porch, everybody with a sweaty glass of tea or a plate heavy with pound cake. Perhaps someone would bring a guitar, someone else a rolled newspaper for mosquitoes. And there they would sit, the whole bunch rowed up on the porch, everyone lazy and immobile, stuffed with fried chicken and creamed potatoes, biscuits and beans. They would talk low, telling jokes or stories or planning the next day's work in the fields. Or maybe they would just sit silently and take in the night — listen to the breeze in the leaves and the chirp and whir of a million insects coming alive on the dark ground beneath a star-speckled sky.

I can see the people now — those from long ago up on a big front porch alongside Chuck Pennington, Shawn Johnson, and my parents. There's the old man from Cedar Island. There's my brother. They cross their legs at the ankles and stir the air with paper fans from a funeral home. The porch swing creaks and groans. They can smell tomorrow's rain.

Finally, when the bugs get too hungry or the humidity too thick, everybody rises, slow and sated, and one by one they leave the front porch and wander inside, ready for sleep.

Pluck one string, and images start forming: rural family gatherings, dirt-floor dances, and simple picking on a porch as the sun sets. Few instruments conjure place more powerfully than the banjo.

WHAT THE BANJO SOUNDS like: a child plucking rubber bands. Rain on a loose tin roof. A spring popping out of a cushion. At times, the banjo can even sound like a human voice, particularly one with a thick Appalachian twang.

More than anything, though, the banjo sounds like the South. The most American of instruments, it is singularly, proudly, and uniquely Southern — accompanied by all resultant glory and complication.

In the 1980s, when I was a boy growing up in North Carolina, the banjo seemed to be the predominant cultural calling card of dimwit hillbillies, thanks in large part to the stereotypical depictions of the "South" in any number of Hollywood products. Can't you hear the banjo ushering the Clampetts into Beverly

Hills? Remember Roy and Buck's "Pickin' and Grinnin'" segments on "Hee Haw?" Or, most unforgettably, the dueling banjos sequence in the film *Deliverance*, when that anemic mountain inbred stares spookily into space while he picks that twangy thing? Could anything have cemented the banjo's late 20th-century status more firmly?

But those representations are far from accurate. Over time, like some cultural chameleon, the banjo has changed its popular identity again and again. I just happened to meet it during a particularly bad stretch. Today, it's changed its colors yet again. Whether played by traditionalists on such albums as the soundtrack to *O Brother, Where Art Thou?* or by such forward-looking innovators as Béla Fleck, the banjo has become the voice of a new generation of Southerners, particularly North Carolinians.

ASHEVILLE'S NEW TRADITION-ALISTS, the Steep Canyon Rangers, have seen their national profile skyrocket after being tapped to back Steve Martin — yes, that Steve Martin — a serious banjo player himself (who just won a Grammy for his 2009 album *The Crow: New Songs for the Five-String Banjo*). Chatham County Line — a four-piece bluegrass band

out of Raleigh that performs around one single-ribbon microphone, like a scene straight out of a 1940s Grand Ole Opry show — has seen its albums scale the charts in, of all places, Norway. Concord's hugely popular Avett Brothers channel rock 'n' roll energy through old-time instrumentation, bringing the banjo to audiences who might otherwise be more entertained by a shoe-gazing electric guitarist. But perhaps no band captures today's evolving banjo identity more than the Carolina Chocolate Drops, an all-black old-time string band based out of Durham.

"There's some surprise," says Dom Flemons, banjo player for the Chocolate Drops. "But coming from this generation now in America, not from that many people. They're listening to the music, not focusing on how I look right off the bat."

Having signed to a major record label and toured the world (while finding time to perform on "A Prairie Home Companion" and establish themselves as darlings of the national press), the Chocolate Drops might have attracted some initial attention for their unique backstory, but the real reason for their success is the most basic of all — it's the music. The same reason Flemons picked up the banjo in the first place.

"I liked the sound of it," he says. "Growing up in the Southwest, there was no cultural divide. I liked playing the instrument and playing songs I enjoyed on it."

Now that he's a resident of North Carolina, the geography has changed his relationship to the instrument.

"The banjo is a sound that evokes another time and place."

"There's a lot more associated with the banjo in the South that I didn't have in Arizona. A lot more of a social consciousness and history," Flemons says. "But the music itself played on the banjo doesn't have to be related on that level. The music itself can become independent of it."

There was a time when that didn't seem so possible.

Descendant from gourd-bodied instruments played throughout Africa, the banjo landed on our shores in the 17th century packed in with the crowded cultural baggage of newly arrived slaves. Scots-Irish landowners who played the fiddle at farm dances soon added it to their repertoires, and

by the 1830s, theaters throughout the North were billing banjo-playing minstrels in blackface portraying "life" on Southern plantations. Their popularity soared, and before long, the banjo became what was essentially a northern, urban instrument.

But despite its popularity in the heavily populated cities of the North, the banjo remained an integral part of indigenous Southern music and folk dancing. By the 1930s, as jazz and ragtime overtook minstrel shows in popularity, North Carolina's Earl Scruggs developed the so-called three-finger technique and soon transformed the way the banjo was played. As bluegrass emerged, the identity of the banjo transitioned to one reconnected to old-time music and the South.

"The banjo comes with certain associations," says Graham Sharp, the bearded young banjo wiz for the Steep Canyon Rangers. "A lot of music has swung back toward more traditional sounds, and the banjo is a sound that evokes another time and place."

It's a time and place that conjures nostalgic visions of rural family gatherings, dirt-floor dances, and simple picking on a porch at sunset. But more than bucolic images, the banjo boasts that sound. The sharp twang, the percussive snap, the stampede of staccato notes. The banjo sounds like nothing else.

A truly primitive instrument, the first banjos were made from wood, animal skin, and string pulled from gut. Even today, the instrument is strange-looking. It has a drum head. It has a neck that looks two sizes too thin. It has one string that doesn't even go all the way to the top. Some have four strings, some five. Some even more than that, but it's the five-string banjo that we think of when we hear bluegrass.

PHILIP GURA, WILLIAM S. NEWMAN DISTINGUISHED Professor of American Literature and Culture at the University of North Carolina at Chapel Hill and co-author of *America's Instrument: The Banjo in the Nineteenth Century* — the definitive book on the banjo — says, "You can't help but smile when you hear a banjo."

And he's right. It's an instrument that's hard to make sound mournful. It's lively, explosive, and still imbued with some of the comic quality left over from its minstrel past. It's still the butt of mediocre jokes: What's the difference between a banjo and a Harley? You can tune a Harley. In fact, Scruggs's three-finger tech-nique — the one most often used in bluegrass playing — actually enhances the instrument's pluck and twang, sounding a singular siren call alerting all listeners that this is an instrument cut from an uncouth swath, one spun from moxie and sass. It's a reputation that's hard to shake.

"The piano may do for love-sick girls who lace themselves to skeletons, and lunch on chalk, pickles, and slate pencils," said Mark Twain. "But give me the banjo. ... When you want genuine music — music that will come right home to you like a bad quarter, suffuse your system like strychnine whisky, go right through you like Brandreth's pills, ramify your whole constitution like the measles, and break out on your hide like the pin-feather pimples on a pickled goose — when you want all of this, just smash your piano and invoke the glory-beaming banjo."

This glory-beaming thing has been drawing more and more fans of late, its growing audience contributing to its constantly evolving identity.

"In the past couple of years, the number of people who have come to old-time music is so much more than even five years ago," says Flemons of the Chocolate Drops. "So people are less surprised to see someone like me playing the banjo because it's more widely accepted on a cultural level. It shows how American culture has changed and the social conflicts around the instrument have changed."

Sharp, of the Steep Canyon Rangers, agrees that the banjo brings together people who might not otherwise cross paths.

"Once I started getting into it," he says, "I started to see a whole subculture of banjo and bluegrass. It's really everywhere, once you know." This community is what kept him interested beyond the initial curiosity that drove him to pick up the banjo in the first place. "You show up at a festival, and if you have a banjo," he says, "you can speak a whole language with other banjo players, whatever their background. It gives you access to a whole shadow-world."

Apparently, this has been part of the banjo's allure for years. Look no further than the 1927 Gibson Banjo catalog for confirmation: "The Gibson Banjo is the modern 'Open Sesame' to a world of good times, fun, and happiness. Ability to play the banjo soon places one in position to pick and choose from scores of social invitation. Everywhere, the banjoist is assured of a hearty welcome."

BUT THE SOUND. More than the community, the history, or the look of the thing, it's the sound that gives the banjo its power. "It's the skip in the heartbeat," says Sharp, alluding to the three-finger pattern played atop the basic four-four bluegrass structure. "It brings about a physical reaction."

Flemons draws a comparison even more intense. "The banjo sounds like a freight train coming around the curve and going right into your face," he says. "But as long as you're not standing in front of the train, you don't have to be afraid."

Maybe so. But here's what the banjo really sounds like: a cascade of sharp and wavering notes plucked out of this region's past and sung continually into its present. It's the weird, complicated, beguiling sound that's ours and no one else's.

It's the unmistakable sound of the South.

CAROLINA

Rails

SOUTHERN

6 81   20 01

by JEREMY MARKOVICH

Long past its prime as the way to travel, a train charging across a field or a city street still has the power to transport us to places beyond its destination.

ONE TIME, Steven Hawkins was rounding the curve in the main line west of Charlotte when he saw something he'd never seen on the railroad before. It was a woman. She was sitting in the middle of the tracks, reading a book. He blew the horn. She moved.

Hawkins has worked for the railroad for 30-some years and even that, the strangest thing he's ever seen from his train, gets only a mild rise out of him. On a Sunday afternoon, he's the conductor on the 212, an 8,565-foot-long caravan of containers carrying postcards, new cars, and chemicals. It left Atlanta early on Sunday and should be in New Jersey sometime Monday evening. Hawkins is responsible for 160 miles of that journey: the stretch from Greenville, South Carolina, to Linwood, North Carolina. He can't tell you how many times he's made the run.

"I know every stone, every tree, every doghouse," he says, chuckling and looking out the window.

He's seen the worst of what you can see from his perch on a Norfolk Southern engine. People have jumped in front of his train. Some folks play chicken, diving off the tracks with seconds to spare. He knows to turn the lights off at night if a deer is on the rails — otherwise, it'll never move.

Hawkins is used to something else: people waving at him. He knows they can't help it. People at crossings wave. People at rail yards wave. People in other trains wave. The conductor and engineer almost always wave back.

HAWKINS SITS ON THE LEFT SIDE of the engine. The engineer on the other side is Steve Mullis, another 30-some-year railroad veteran who grew up in Marshville and had a high school class with Randy Travis once. Mullis is the driver. There are two computer monitors in front of him, along with bulky plastic levers within reach to control the throttle and the brakes. There's a silvery knob near the top of one panel. Mullis taps it with the same cadence, long-long-short-long, whenever he comes to a crossing. Each tap blows the horn.

In front of Hawkins are four things: a speedometer, an emergency brake, a horn, and a radio. His eyes are usually on the tracks ahead, looking for something treacherous on the rails. He scans passing trains for damage or open doors. He cranes his neck to see what's coming around the next corner. When there's nothing, he simply says, "clear."

Trains are more than mighty. They are time machines.

Hawkins is a few years away from retirement, at which time the constant four-days-on, one-day-off rhythm of a conductor's life will end. He's thinking of going on a cruise with his wife. Brazil, maybe.

At the end of his runs to Linwood, when Norfolk Southern puts him up at the Country Hearth Inn in Lexington (the railroad rents the whole third floor for workers), Hawkins hits the gym. Hard. It is a way of killing time before he rides the 213 home to Spartanburg, South Carolina, the next day. His chiseled arms stretch the sleeves on his olive-colored T-shirt. He is powerful, much like the yellow locomotive he sits on, a strong man to match the 4,000-horse-power engine beneath.

Trains are more than mighty. They are time machines. With a glance, they take you back to the era of cabooses, firemen, and coal cars. They are colorful and brash, arriving and departing to a time when getting there was fraught with adventure and hardship. The tracks themselves have their own personality — steel rails and creosote-soaked railroad ties running through Blue Ridge tunnels and across eastern rivers on trestles. The W-Line hugs the Broad River. The A-Line goes straight over hills. On Old Fort Mountain, the rails wind around the slope in such a way that, on your way down, you can look straight up from the locomotive and see the rear of your train above you. Trains don't just take you to a destination. They are the destination.

TRAVEL USED TO BE TERRIBLE, back when it took damn near forever to get anywhere because there were no trains. If you had the misfortune of needing to make it from Wilmington to New York City in 1800, you were doomed to a week of riding a boat or, worse, a stagecoach. North Carolina's ports were too shallow, its rivers too rapid, and its roads boggy and rutted enough to swallow half a wagon wheel. The biggest cities were once exclusively on the coast because it was just too hard for too many people

to make it to the Piedmont, let alone the mountains. Trains changed that.

By 1840, North Carolina had two railroads, which ran north-south, and suddenly the Rip Van Winkle State woke up, and the steam engines started puffing and pulled in all sorts of stuff from factories in the North and sent the Yankees cotton and tobacco in return, exporting our Southernness to faraway places. It was still hard to get from east to west. Some lawmakers decided to fix that and, in the 1850s, paid for a set of tracks from Charlotte to Goldsboro. They called it the North Carolina Railroad, which, even today, is owned by the state, is still used by Norfolk Southern, and runs parallel to Interstate 85 from Charlotte to Durham.

By 1860, the once weeklong Wilmington-to-New York trip took only two days by train. Railroads fanned out, their routes spreading like capillaries across the North while North Carolina was left with a few spider veins. When the Civil War began, Southern factories were much too busy making ammo to make more tracks, and when General Sherman rolled through here after burning Atlanta, he decided to make a mangled mess of the Carolina railroads. In 1865, Chief Justice Salmon P. Chase toured North Carolina, doing so in a train described as "a wheezy little locomotive and an old mail car with the windows smashed and half the seats gone." Early train tracks were built with strap iron rails, which tended to come loose and bend upward over time, sometimes cutting up into and through the floor of coach cars — a bit unfortunate for you if you happened to be riding in one.

THERE IS SAMUEL SPENCER, namesake of Spencer, a small Rowan County town, who was the first and arguably best president the Southern Railway ever had. In 1906, he died in the most eerily appropriate way. He was hit by a train. There is James B. Duke, the tobacco titan who also became the Duke in Duke University and Duke Energy. He became fond of riding the rails, so much so that in 1917, he bought his own private Pullman passenger car, named it Doris for his daughter, loaded it up with gin and cigars, and took it everywhere from New York to Florida. Once, Duke needed to convince some state lawmakers to stay out of his power company's affairs. He took the swing votes on a ride in the Doris. They left him alone after that.

Trains were romantic. Stylish. Sexy. Asheville's Thomas Wolfe was smitten by the night train. "It is the place," he wrote in *Of Time and The River*, "where women with fine legs and silken underwear lie in the Pullman berth below you." Even today, locomotives have an Art Deco look. Their discordant whistles still echo through the night. You can close your eyes and imagine a streamlined diesel hauling freight, or a steam locomotive pulling passengers. You don't need to see it. With just a whistle, the possibilities are endless.

Trains aren't just syrupy-sweet nostalgia. For every quaint story of life in a tiny whistle-stop town, there are stories of mergers and bankruptcies, of dirt and grime and broken rails and lost money. For every romantic story about a locomotive running through the night, there is an annual meeting of worried railroad stockholders.

Take C.E. Spear, who speaks in that decidedly Southern way, replacing his Rs with uhs and using the word "why" exclusively for emphasis. He likes trains. Doesn't love 'em. Just likes 'em. He ended up in Rowan County in 1942 because his brother was already there, already working for the Southern Railway. He took a job as a boilermaker, beating on steel all day in a sooty repair shop in Spencer, sucking smoke into his lungs, losing his hearing.

"Back in those days, why, we didn't even have earplugs," Spear says, drawling the word ear into ea-yuh. "We used cotton balls."

Was it a good job? Why, yes. The old steam engines depended on firemen to shovel coal and gulped down water every 150 miles or so. They belched out smoke and broke down, bad for the railroad companies but good for boilermakers like C.E. Spear. There was nothing romantic about it. "It was just a livin'," he says.

Dependable diesel engines, like the ones at the head of the 212, replaced the misbehaving steam locomotives. Diesels could go farther (1,000 miles without refueling) and had no need for brakemen, firemen, and the like. In 1960, after 18 years, C.E. Spear found himself looking for a new job. Why pay a boilermaker if there aren't any boilers to fix?

TODAY, PASSING TRAIN CARS can be eerily silent. The clickety-clack is gone because the rails on Norfolk Southern's main lines are welded together into one continuous piece of metal. People do not ride on trains to get anywhere they need to be, unless they have a lot of spare time, which they tend not to. There is no such thing as a runaway train anymore. On the 212, if the engineer doesn't wiggle a switch or touch a button every 90 seconds, the computer hits the brakes.

There is, then, surprisingly little that really goes on in the cab of a modern train. On the 212, Hawkins and Mullis sit calmly. They make small adjustments to levers. They lightly tap the horn. Mostly, they look out the windows to see North Carolina roll by.

Heading into Bessemer City, Hawkins and Mullis try to guess exactly how hot it is before they pass by the bank with the time and temperature on the sign. In Cramerton, the tracks are so high up, the 212 is at steeple-level with the Riverside Baptist Church. In Belmont, some of the old-timers open up lawn chairs and point them at the tracks, just to watch the trains go by on Sundays. In Charlotte, the railroad passes within yards of the airport tarmac. It sneaks in behind Bank of America Stadium.

By the afternoon, Hawkins and Mullis stop their locomotive in the middle of a green field outside of Linwood. They call this the farmer's crossing. Their replacements, sitting on the side of an asphalt berm, rise to their feet. There will be five or six more crew changes before the 212 reaches its destination. A hired minivan will take Hawkins off to the hotel after his shift. He'll work out tonight. He'll be back home tomorrow. His wife understands. She works for the railroad, too.

The sun is out, and the crew swings the heavy door open at the nose of the locomotive. They climb down in their fluorescent yellow vests, an unnatural color among the green grass and blue sky. They turn back to see the new crew up on the engine. The bells clang. The horn blares.

They wave.

Long after Junior Johnson famously learned to drive hauling outlaw liquor, distillers are again providing the fiery flavor of the backwoods — all with the state's blessing.

I KNOW A GUY who knows a guy. It took 25 bucks and the sense not to ask any questions. We made a discreet transaction at the end of a party. I bootlegged it home in the trunk of my Toyota. One quart of homemade peach moonshine — North Carolina in a jar.

We'll talk more in a second. But first, take a sip.

Don't gulp it — you'll be spitting and snorting half the night. Just let a little bit slide between your lips. That peeled peach, looking like Mars floating around in there, sands off some of the hard edge. You might even taste the fruit first. But right behind it comes the fire. It's not a big roaring flame like the old days — that old 140-proof white lightning is hard to find anymore. This is more like 80. Like a big stack of oak burned down to the coals.

That taste, right there, helped build our state. It helped define our history. It helped create our most famous export.

And today, it still thrives.

Occasionally, it's even legal.

IN THE TOWN OF MADISON, north of Greensboro near the Virginia line, two giant oak barrels crowd one end of a long, narrow room in the old train depot. Each barrel is filled with 135 gallons of mash — a mix of corn, yeast, and water that's been fermenting for three days. It looks like thin buttermilk and smells like wet grass clippings. Some old-timers call it beer and drink it just like this. But this mash is headed for the still. And this particular still happens to have government permits.

It belongs to Piedmont Distillers, which began making moonshine for commercial sale in 2005. Its two brands — Catdaddy and Midnight Moon — are now sold in 32 states. On a recent weekday morning, while the mash aged at one end of the room, workers packed fresh raspberries into finished 'shine at the other. You can now get Midnight Moon in seven fruit flavors.

The pots in Piedmont's main still are made of stainless steel, instead of the copper in the typical backwoods still. And these pots are big — the main vessel holds 500 gallons, where a regular still's pot might hold 50. But the process is about the same as it ever was. The mash goes into the main pot and cooks to 173 degrees — the temperature at which alcohol vapors start to boil off. Those vapors are piped into a second pot, called a thumper keg, where they cook again to get rid of impurities. Then the vapors go into a condenser, through spiraled copper tubing (the worm) surrounded by cold water. The cold turns the vapors back into liquid. Hold a jar under the spout, and soon enough, you'll get moonshine.

BRIAN CALL, THE MASTER distiller at Piedmont, traces his family back to Dan Call, the man who taught Jack Daniel how to make whiskey. The trade has carried through several generations — Brian's dad partnered in the moonshine business with Junior Johnson, the legendary NASCAR driver who smuggled moonshine out of Wilkes County. "My dad got sent to prison for whiskey," Brian says. "It's a lot easier to do it the legal way."

Johnson is a partner and shareholder in the distillery, and his name is on the Midnight Moon bottle. But the guy behind the operation is a New York native named Joe Michalek. He moved to North Carolina in 1995 to market tobacco companies. That meant a lot of races and a lot of music festivals. And at just about every one, he noticed, somebody would pull out a Mason jar.

"Some of it was terrible," he says.

Moonshine helped build what we think of as Carolina culture.

"But some of it was so good I started wondering why nobody was making this commercially. So I started looking into it. And the deeper I got into it, the more I realized how much moonshine is a part of the Carolina culture."

In fact, moonshine helped build what we think of as Carolina culture — especially Carolina mountain culture. Scots-Irish immigrants poured down into the North Carolina mountains from Pennsylvania and Virginia in the 1700s looking for cheap land and freedom from authority. Many brought the whiskey-making skills they learned across the Atlantic. And even teetotaler farmers figured out that corn was easier to haul to market — and brought a lot more money — in liquid form.

The problem was taxes. The new United States government decided to levy taxes on liquor in 1791 to help pay off Revolutionary War debts. Distillers fought back in a movement that came to be called the Whiskey Rebellion. The rebellion ended quietly three years later, with the government in charge, but the most determined moonshiners pushed back deeper into the woods and kept cooking.

Moonshine built legends. Amos Owens of Rutherford County, west of Charlotte, became famous throughout the South for his "cherry bounce" — a blend of corn whiskey, sourwood honey, and cherry juice. His operation made untold thousands of barrels from the 1840s through 1890, except for a stint during the Civil War. Moonshine made Owens enough money to buy Cherry Mountain, where the fruit for his bounce grew wild. It also got him arrested and jailed again and again. In his last court appearance, at age 68, a judge in Charlotte looked him over and said: "Amos, man to man, will you cease to violate the laws of our country and be an outcast of society?" Amos answered through tears: "Judge, I'll try." And he never made another jug. At least that's how the story goes.

IN SOME WAYS, THE WORST THING that happened to moonshine was Prohibition. Big-time criminals moved into the illegal-liquor business. Most didn't care much about quality. And even some established moonshiners cut corners to meet the high demand. They skipped the thumper kegs and charcoal filters that got rid of fusel oils — the byproducts that give bad moonshine a solvent smell (and also cause wicked hangovers). Sometimes, they just didn't pay enough attention. My daddy, who grew up in Georgia in the '20s and '30s, remembered running across a still on a hunting trip and spotting a dead squirrel floating in the mash. But once Prohibition ended in 1933, most of the short-timers cleared out, and most of the rotgut did, too.

(This is probably a good time to pause and acknowledge that moonshine is not sweet tea, and even the best of it is not to be trifled with. Alcohol abuse has ruined lives and broken homes. In all things, moderation.)

By the time Prohibition ended, moonshiners had traded their horses and wagons for cars. They modified the cars for whiskey hauling, hollowing out the interiors for storage, tweaking the engines for power. The '39 flathead Ford, with ample room and a powerful V8 engine, became the moonshiner's car of choice. Before long, between bootlegging runs, some folks decided to see whose car was fastest.

Jimmie Lewallen was one of those folks. Growing up around High Point, he delivered moonshine on his motorcycle, the cargo tucked in his saddlebags. By the late '30s, he was racing cars, first in fields, then on dirt tracks. He went off to World War II and jumped back into race cars when he got back. He was one of the first drivers in what ended up becoming NASCAR. A bunch of NASCAR's early stars learned their skills by outrunning revenuers. There's a nod to that history at the NASCAR Hall of Fame in Charlotte — up on the fourth level, you can find a replica of one of Junior Johnson's old stills. He put it together himself.

Jimmie Lewallen died in 1995. His son, Gary, thought his dad's story might make a good movie someday. So Gary raised $600,000 and financed the movie *Red Dirt Rising*. It's not a documentary, but it's basically Jimmie's story. And along the way, it's the story of moonshine and NASCAR and North Carolina.

"Moonshine, for him, was about opportunity and money," Gary says. "But also the chase, going out here running liquor up and down the road. There's a group of people that have always been around North Carolina. … It's right on the edge of being a bad guy, but not totally. There's a twofold thing there. Always has been."

Jimmie was out of the moonshine business by the time Gary grew up. And here's that twofold thing: Gary went into law enforcement. He spent more than 30 years on the job, retiring as police chief of Archdale in 2009. Along the way, he busted up a few moonshine stills. He once found a still outside of Thomasville, got an engineer to put some dynamite under it, and invited a TV crew. It blew the still 100 feet into the air.

"I always told everybody I had three choices for a career," Gary says. "Race. Run liquor. Or the police department. I got the one with the better retirement plan."

MAKING MOONSHINE HAS NEVER been an easy life. That's part of the North Carolina story, too — people worked hard here, whether it was cropping tobacco or pulling the graveyard shift at a textile mill. Plus, of course, most moonshiners lived on the other side of the law.

"We wasn't stealing — we was dodging," Junior Johnson says. "Back when I was doing it, you could make a gallon of whiskey for a dollar and sell it for 3 or 4 dollars. But the government wanted 11 dollars a gallon in taxes. You couldn't make no money that way."

But now Piedmont Distillers is making a go of it. And up around Asheville, Troy Ball is about to give it a shot.

She and her husband — both real-estate developers — moved to Asheville from Austin, Texas, seven years ago. They bought some land in Madison County, met some people up there. Time after time, folks stopping by would bring her a jar to taste. She wouldn't even try it at first. But then she took a sip that was so smooth, and she wanted to make it herself.

So now she does. She partnered with Highland Brewing Co., a craft-beer brewer, to build a moonshine distillery in Asheville. She uses heirloom white corn for the mash. And her plan is to have Troy and Sons Moonshine on the shelves this summer.

"What I found is that people will tell you their secrets about moonshine, as long as they know you're not a threat to them," she says. "These guys don't just embrace anybody right off. But they're proud of what they make. The world needs to know there's such a thing as quality moonshine."

That's a fact. You can still get a drink of moonshine, legal or otherwise, that's not a whole lot different than what they were drinking when this country was founded. There's a lot of history in that jar. Go ahead, take another sip. It's for sharing.

SPANISH
Moss

by MICHAEL PARKER

Trees along our state's eastern edge
drape themselves in the shadowy moss
indelibly linked to the Old South.

I'M NOT SURE WHERE Spanish moss makes its first appearance in the trees of Sampson County, but I can pinpoint a place in Clinton where I first came upon it. My high school English teacher, a close friend of the family, lived a couple miles west of town. Her house sat off the road among orderly rows of pines. Moss hung from the limbs, and one Halloween I picked up a fallen tress, tucked it into my father's crimped fedora, and roamed the streets dressed, in those pre-politically correct days, as a bum. I'm not sure what led me to believe that bums sprouted wild, gray dread-locks, but I do remember the feel of the moss on the back of my neck and its smell, which after a few hours trolling neighborhoods for sweets, resembled washed-up seaweed you pluck from the beach and decide to take home with you, until — after an hour or two in the car with the windows rolled up — you realize that some forms of nature are best left in nature.

As dean of students at the local community college, my mother traveled the county recruiting high school students. Often she took my brother and sister and me along. Even in elementary school, I sensed the difference in the southern end of the county. We'd take two tracks of thick, white sand through scrubby woods of cypress and oak. On saggy cabins, cotton balls studded porch and front-door screens to ward off flies. Overhead, the tree limbs seemed about to snap under the weight of the exotic Spanish moss.

There is something primitive, even prehistoric, about the plant, not to mention haunting.

SPANISH MOSS IS NEITHER Spanish nor, technically, moss. It belongs to the angiosperm family and, according to one legend, got its name from a tale about an 18th-century couple — a man and his Spanish fiancé — who, searching for a place to build a plantation near Charleston, South Carolina, were attacked by Cherokees. After killing the couple, the Cherokees cut off the Spanish woman's long, black tresses and tossed them onto the branch of a live oak, where they turned gray and spread across the Southeast. Over time, Spanish moss became a fixture of the Southern Gothic, and even now crops up in movies set in the South made mostly by outsiders who portray the region with easy stereotypes and overwrought accents.

Moonlight, magnolias, and moss: symbols of a mysterious and arcane region where the past, as Faulkner famously said, is never dead; it is not even past. There is something primitive, even prehistoric, about the plant, not to mention haunting. Over the years, it developed its own vocabulary. It drapes, and it drips; it never droops or dangles. That the verbs used to describe the way it hangs have been worn threadbare only attests to its place of honor in our landscape, for clichés, however bland and tired, are born out of truth. In truth, Spanish moss drips from trees. Branches are draped with it. Beards, tresses, locks: We anthropomorphize it because — even though it appears not only dead but decades dead, even centuries — it lives, vibrantly, in our identity.

Wind or nesting birds spread it from tree to tree, but compared to kudzu, another stock symbol of the Southern Gothic, which does not so much spread as devour, it's hard to imagine Spanish moss not having always been here. Maybe its grayness renders it antediluvian. All I know is that years ago, when I first came upon it as a child, it felt alive in the Now but a harbinger of Then.

YEARS OF LIVING EITHER out of state or in the moss-deprived Piedmont have made me nostalgic for it. Last year, on my daughter's spring break from the University of North Carolina at Chapel Hill, I suggested a pilgrimage down east. My daugh-

ter had never really seen Sampson County, except to drive through it on the way to the beach. Unlike most college students who are asked to spend spring break riding around in a Toyota with their dad and listening to him wax nostalgic about nights listening to the Tams and the Drifters at Lake Artesia and working in the old produce market in Faison, she actually appeared eager, if not fascinated.

We headed out from Greensboro down U.S. Highway 421, for interstates are the enemy of exploration. A couple of hours later, driving the length of Sampson County, we passed from tobacco field and pine forest a few miles outside of Dunn, to the sunken, swampy lushness of Ivanhoe, on the banks of the Black River. Perhaps the most noticeable aspect of the largest county in the state is the fact that, like most states, it includes different landscapes and ecosystems.

Even its wildlife is different: North of Clinton you find deer and copperheads, but I can remember from my long-lost youth a photo on the front page of the newspaper my father once owned of a sheriff's deputy holding a rattlesnake as long as a rake found down around Garland. Black bears have been spotted roaming the swamps of lower Sampson. Once, when my Boy Scout troop went camping down on the Black, we were advised to purchase stiff canvas gaiters from an army surplus store to protect our shins from the deadly bite of the tiny and beautifully banded coral snake.

I HAVE ALWAYS preferred that end of the county to the flat and crop-dominated land north of Clinton. Down south, little of the land is cleared; the roads are limned by shadow from the overhanging trees, the scrub nearly impenetrable. From Ivanhoe, my daughter and I took a side road down to Kerr Station. Past a bridge over the Black River, we pulled into a parking lot, doubtless improvised by fishermen. But, except for us, no one was around that day in early spring. The river was quiet and slow, its waters tannic-laced, more the color of cola when you're standing beside it, but certainly black from a distance.

Cypress trees dominated the banks, their knees creating eddies in the barely perceptible current. From their branches hung the first moss we'd seen that day, and it was everywhere overhead, thick and moody.

"Check out that moss. I love it, don't you?" I said. The sight of it, still on that windless day, made me oversell it.

From their branches hung the first moss we'd seen that day, and it was everywhere overhead, thick and moody.

"Kind of creepy," she said.

"But in a good way, right?"

"Right, Dad," she said, as if she sensed in my exuberance a need to make her appreciate it.

I told her about the times, back when we lived in Elizabeth City, when she was 2 years old, when we drove over to Gates County and rented canoes to paddle around Merchants Millpond, the trees of which are so laden with moss it seems impossible that they are standing. And the next day, we passed through the Green Swamp and stopped at Lake Waccamaw, another place where moss is more abundant.

But what I could not seem to communicate was how much I preferred the Spanish moss of lower Sampson.

It comes upon you suddenly, and it seems that you're not only moving from one habitat to another, but also from the present into the past. And that is exactly where I was headed that day.

I suspect the sight of moss will always usher me backward, and in a good way, too.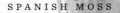

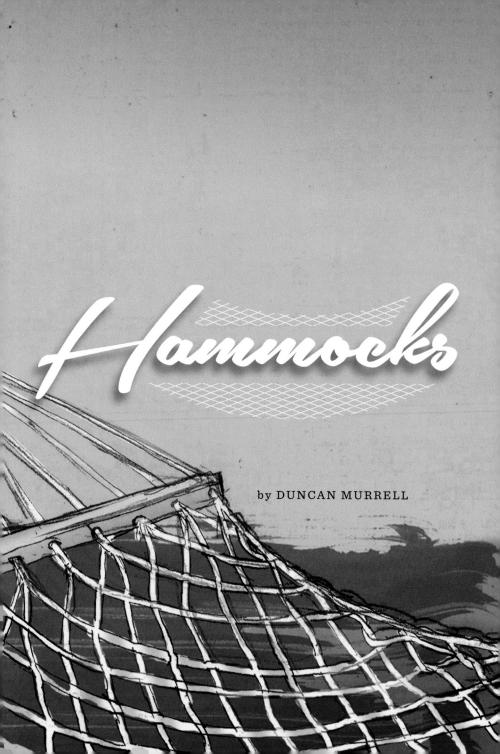

Hammocks

by DUNCAN MURRELL

A hammock does not yield easily to our impulse to rush off. Enforcing a slow, Southern pace, its knotted web cradles us, convincing us it's better to stay put for a while longer.

IN A CLEARING AMONG the oaks of Salter Path, there is a hammock, and upon this hammock, I once dreamed that time had expanded and become nearly infinite even for as small a mortal speck of creation as me, and that I would have all the time I needed to get out of that hammock and on down to Frost Seafood House for breakfast. It was good that I had all the time I needed, that each second had swelled to encompass the growing universe and all of its comets and suns, that time was, like, dude, the sand trail of that little crab right there, winding and twisting back on itself in the endless circle of … oh man, look at that big pelican, he's so weird.

I was having a hard time getting out of the hammock is what I'm trying to say. I don't mean that I was reluctant to get out of the hammock. I was hungry and needed eggs to fuel my later study of hammock aerodynamics and nap engineering, scheduled for immediately after breakfast. When I say I had a hard time getting out, I mean that I could not physically remove myself from the thing. The hammock had closed up around me, as hammocks do; I had a vision of dying to the world within its precisely knotted and airy shroud for want of a graceful way to get out. The hammock would not let me go unless I was prepared to utterly reject it for terra firma, which meant dumping myself out onto the sandy soil at the feet of the windswept oaks.

I assume I did this, eventually, as I am not still in the hammock, and I recount this moment, one of hundreds of my hammock moments, only to illustrate the first principle of hammockology, which is: You must commit to the hammock. The hammock will not let you go easily. It isn't a bed or a couch, from which you can leap up at a moment's notice to attend to the world. A hammock demands that it be given time, and the best kind of time is leisure time, as we all know.

SOUTHERNERS HAVE LONG FOUGHT the idea that they are innately lazy. What this Southerner prefers to think is that he is unusually capable of commitment to leisure. He is not undecided about the

The Southerner is not afraid of the hammock because the Southerner is not afraid of time.

merits of sitting still, and he doesn't need a guru or a life coach to tell him that a gentle rocking in the breeze is worth setting aside the concerns of the world. The magazines shout at him: SIMPLIFY NOW! 10 THINGS YOU MUST DO TO LOWER STRESS TODAY! He considers these imperatives, but they only make him want to close his eyes and, Hey, there's that pelican again. And the crab, silly thing.

THE SOUTHERNER IS NOT afraid of the hammock because the Southerner is not afraid of time. The Southerner's sense of time is expansive; it stretches across the centuries and takes in the panoply of souls that rose, animate, blood kin and not, venerated and despised, chained and unchained, a people divided against itself, one people of the twang, an operatic chorus describing the strange fruit of their long history together. The Southerner is conscious of eons, and against that scale of time, each second is nothing, a flash, and not anything that must always be crammed full. We will all be dust, the Southerner knows, so the Southerner stops, the Southerner remembers, the Southerner falls asleep in the hammock with Mr. Wolfe's novel butterflied on his chest, vaguely aware of the rough lattice of thread and fiber pressed against his cheek, and he dreams: I am always home, sir, and I am always going there, too.

Down those centuries, the hammock accompanied us: from the New World, where we found them strung up by the first people high above the leaf litter and biting ants of the tropical forest, to the Old World and back again, below decks where sailors slept steadily rocking, bearded and grog-happy pendula always oriented in line with gravity and never tossed out upon the deck. Blackbeard surely slept in a hammock, it being impossible to imagine the old captain at sea laid down in anything so domestic as a bed.

I am a hammock enthusiast, and therefore the descendant of pirates and privateers, a free man floating weightless above the entanglements of ground and soil. You may keep your pied-à-terre; I will carry my resting place with me.

In fact, I want to unfurl it right now. The very idea of essaying about a hammock has made me sleepy, and it has not escaped me that tap-tap-tapping at this keyboard is nearly the opposite of resting in a hammock. I might as well be swinging a hammer:

That nine pound hammer that killed John Henry,

Ain't a gonna kill me, ain't a gonna kill me.

Roll on buddy, don't you roll so slow.

Baby how can I roll, when the wheels won't go?

It won't kill me because I'll be asleep and not trying to tunnel through a mountain in a race against a machine. The machines lost that particular battle against old hardworking and restless John Henry, but does anyone really doubt they won the war? I will not fight them, but at times I will ignore them.

I will instead go outside into the shade behind the old house in Beaufort, beyond the sound of the air conditioner and the refrigerator and the electric sandwich maker. And I will tie up my hammock with my own fat fingers from the crooked branches of asymmetrical old trees and allow myself to be cooled, supine, in the breeze that has blown across that same inlet since before the first man stood up, became self-aware, and began to look for shade and a cool drink.

THIS IS THE SOUTHERNER'S sense of time: breezes are ancient, and hammocks are so simple they're subversive. This simplicity, this rudimentary perfection, is worth preserving. One must reject all manner of tassels and fringe. The spreader bars of the local hammock variants are acceptable, those types native to Nags Head and Hatteras. The important rule, though, is that the hammock should retain its primitivity; otherwise you're building yourself a bed, and that's just a quick step from getting a mortgage.

Just for one hour once during the week you grudgingly allow yourself for vacation, would it kill you to be

The hammock invites us to quit worrying. It is simple, it is old, it is portable. It is perfect.

irresponsible and not so securely fastened to the things of this world? Forget what your stuff looks like, and who designed it, and whether it's the same brand as that thing in that movie with the lighthouses and the sand and the pretty people. There are some things that invite us to set aside such worries, that are so simple — a sling between two trees! — that to embellish them is to miss the point entirely.

Whether woven from braided unicorn hair or fashioned from a set of old curtains strung up with grappling hooks and jumper cables, the hammock invites us to quit worrying. It will not let us go easily. It is simple, it is old, it is portable. It is perfect, and there's always one to be found in those places where people think it is perfectly fine to stop and consider, at length, the twisting thread of time that has not culminated in us, but is ours only for this moment.

This is North Carolina, this is why we live here. There is no elongation of the space-time continuum here, and time is the same as it is everywhere else. But even so, doesn't it seem sometimes, when you're in your backyard in the ratty old hammock your family has condemned as unsafe, counting willow oak leaves as they spin on their longitudinal axis down slight hills of air toward you, vaguely hearing your daughters playing their ancient games of mimicry — doesn't it seem, then, that there's just more time here? You must commit to the hammock.

Never in my house was it, "Let's go for a ride." Always — and impromptu, although ever-anticipated on those steamy, buggy late-summer nights or languorous Sunday afternoons of my youth — my father said, when he was ready to ramble about town and through countryside, "Let's go to ride."

IT DID NOT OCCUR TO ME then to question his choice of preposition. I wasn't studying linguistics in elementary school. How he happened to martial his troops was immaterial, for I'd been waiting all day — sometimes all weekend — to hear those strange but familiar words, to climb in that car with my parents and some or all of my siblings, and go for an aimless cruise.

I say aimless, but there was a pattern, faint and ever-shifting as it might have been. We'd head from our house two miles from the center of Clinton, up the Faircloth Freeway, the new stretch of four lane named for a local boy turned state senator, and hang a right on N.C. Highway 24 toward Fayetteville. A mile or so in, past what we called, for reasons I could only assume had to do with a preponderance of Johnsons, Johnsontown, we'd veer off into the back entrance of the Coharie Country Club. Back in the late '60s and early '70s, sandy, cockleburred lots thick with pine trees that covered the soil year-round with pine straw were being snapped up by people who could afford to live on the seventh hole of the only golf course in the county. Roads — mostly cul-de-sacs — cropped up in a matter of weeks, flags marking property lines, cement mixers poised to lay the foundation of a French Provincial or Charleston Low Country-style cottage tucked up along a fairway. The country club, essentially a loop, was an easy cruise, and an obligatory one. The main road skirted the greens and fairways, the putting green and pro shop, then dumped us back out on 24.

Across the street from the country club was a newer development, named Fox Lake after the residents it displaced, although there were fox sightings as late as the mid-'70s. The road circled the man-made lake, and my father and mother studied the housing starts or already-completed brick ranchers and told stories about who lived there, where they had lived previously, how many children they had, what line of work they were in, sometimes what church they belonged to.

New neighborhoods were infinitely more explorable than the older and more familiar sections hugging the courthouse square, for they suggested growth in a town where the population — about 7,000 — had remained the same for some time. Progress and prosperity were important to my father, the editor of the local newspaper, and my mother, dean of students of the local community college. Even though they weren't natives, they had an investment in the community, for they were the types to invest in the community.

BUT GOING TO RIDE was not work; it was leisure. That was the point — to get out of the house, to open the car windows wide in those pre-air-conditioned days and whip up a summer breeze, to wander. Rides were also entertainment, fodder for stories. My father could not pass a house without doling out an anecdote about its inhabitants. My mother knew as much as he did about who lived where and did what, but she was the daughter of a Presbyterian minister, so she was a little tighter with the reins of what her father might have deemed idle chatter. That so many of our rides took place on Sunday afternoon suggested to me, much later, that going to ride was a secular extension of the morning of worship. If true religion requires a vigilant attentiveness to the world around you, its changes and its failings, going to ride was a journey through examples — of the beauty of nature, of the occasional sign of greed, of the duty emphasized by more enlightened churches to the community.

We witnessed poverty, too, on those rides. My father took us through the backstreets — unpaved and potholed — of what was then called, by the white population, without the slightest awareness or shame, Colored Town. The divide between Main Street, with its regal Victorians and antebellum oaks, and the side streets off McKoy or Sampson streets — shotguns and unpainted mill shacks, weedy lots and abandoned vehicles — was obvious and instructive. So maybe those rides weren't only leisure, or entertainment. Our parents taught by example, and they did not try to hide us from the world's ills. They were not the type — and still aren't — to lecture. They were the type to question the world around them and their children's place in that world. Not having an answer to their question was not likely to draw a rebuke, for they realize that for most of society's ills, there are no easy answers and the answers that come to you are often ephemeral. But the questions they plant are finally more powerful than any answer, for questions, unlike answers, are niggling — they remain within you, nagging, begging you to reconsider, to adapt, to accept and enact change.

BUT BACK THEN, I just knew that we were getting in a station wagon and going To Ride. Sometimes on summer nights, the city truck we called the Mosquito Man cruised the streets spraying a thick plume of DDT. We had the sense to roll up the windows, more because of the smell than the fact that we were breathing poison (although no one knew that then, as attested by the way that the Mosquito Man's vehicle often looked like the fire truck in a downtown parade, a string of cars following along as if in celebration of homecoming or holiday). Sometimes you even saw neighborhood kids tailing the truck, as Rodney Crowell describes in his song "Telephone Road": "Mosquito Trucks spraying DDT/Barefoot heathens running wild and free."

After we exhausted the town roads, we broke into the country. There wasn't exactly a transition, for most roads out of town were overtaken immediately after the last house or country store by tobacco, corn, or produce fields. Country drives were slightly less interesting to me as a child; there seemed less to look at, for I had not yet cottoned to the barren beauty of field and pine forest that is eastern North Carolina. In time, however, they would come to fascinate and placate me. At some point in high school, my friend Sam and I took long drives, mostly through the southern end of the county. On my rides with Sam, I discovered the dilatory and slightly gothic Black River, fishing shacks tucked up along its banks. We'd drive to Ivanhoe and Harrell's Store and Kerr Station on a rainy Sunday, and the muddy, stubbled cornfields and the line of pines ringing them, softened in the distance by steady drizzle, brought on a melancholy I mistook for profundity. It was then, and is now in memory, akin to some foreign explorer seeing for the first time the beauty of a region at first glance not particularly comely. Those rides with Sam, who passed away some years ago, taught me to see the place I grew up in, to understand its culture, to marvel at the old farmhouses wrestled to the ground by kudzu, the tobacco barns constructed of logs chinked with concrete idle now that farmers cure their crops in metal boxes.

But these being high school days, most of our rides stayed within the city limits. How many times have I heard, talking to others about their experience growing up in small North Carolina towns, that, "There wasn't anything to do but ride around?" We got our driver's licenses and joined the circuit of "cruisers" making their loops around town. These days, small towns are relished by those escaping suburbs who complain about being too often

What I mostly remember from my adolescence is the inordinate amount of time I spent "riding around."

stuck on freeways or spending hours planning routes designed to avoid getting stuck on freeways. Small towns feel idyllic because you can get away from car culture — you can walk to the grocery store, the farmers market, the drugstore, the diner. We could easily have walked to Butler's drugstore for a cherry Coke, or to the Colonial or A&P or the Piggly Wiggly.

But we spent nearly all our time in cars. I remember watching some television, and I remember listening to a lot of records, but what I mostly remember from my adolescence is the inordinate amount of time I spent "riding around." If half your life is spent asleep, for rural North Carolinians of a certain age, the other half is spent in perpetual orbit designed by your particular clique. In Clinton, in the mid-1970s, a certain type of teen — girls with elaborate, shag haircuts; boys with blown-dry, unnaturally kempt hair, flowered, silk shirts, and platform shoes — halted their circling to hang out in the parking lot of Hardee's. Another crowd broke their loop at McDonald's. My crowd hung out, believe it or not, in the parking lot of a Laundromat called The Glam-O-Rama. This was around the time that David Bowie and T. Rex popularized the glitzy, theatrical brand of music called Glam Rock, but The Glam-O-Rama had nothing to do with glitz. It was open late, and drew tired-looking women who moved as if they had worked double shifts, their cars sunken with laundry and so many small kids that half of them had to have been cousins. We liked it because there were two pinball machines, and the management left us alone and most of our high school had too much respect to break their orbit in a sad Laundromat, thus allowing us a kind of refuge from which to judge those we called the Hardee Boys, who listened only to Boz Scaggs and drove Monte Carlos and Grand Prixs instead of the station wagons and pickups we borrowed from our parents.

THERE IS A PHOTO, somewhere, of my mother and father on a back road of Chatham County. My father is standing on a rise above the car — which looks to be a station wagon from the early '50s — taking a photo both of the landscape and of my mother, who, still seated in the passenger's seat, is turned toward him with one of the most beatific smiles I've ever seen, on her face or anyone else's. I can't glance at that photo without tasting kicked-up dust — a briny flavor peculiar to the red clay of the Piedmont — and smell the metal of that part of station wagons we christened the Very Back, which oddly enough was coveted among the five of us, perhaps because you could see the world after it passed through the vision of those up front, allowing you time to savor the sky, like a pot of Brunswick stew that tastes better as a leftover.

I asked my father about that photo the other day, trying to determine where it was taken and why he was there. "I couldn't tell you where, but I could take you there," he said, which told me all I needed to know about the place: that he and my mother discovered it one afternoon while going to ride, and that the look on my mother's face reflects the pleasure experienced when you find something beautiful made all the more mysterious by the fact that you weren't looking for it.

LIGHTNIN'
Bugs

by DIANE SUMMERVILLE

Fireflies lure us down from our porches and lead us on an easy chase. In western North Carolina, encountering the blue ghost firefly takes a little more effort.

I N TOTAL DARKNESS, eyes don't adjust. Blackness stays black. Josh Rosen stands about a foot away from me. I know this only because he's talking. "A little bit of rain is a good thing. They prefer moist environments. But if it's raining very hard, they won't come out. The raindrops will knock them down."

Rosen, an environmental scientist and our expert on this night in late May, is telling the group gathered in DuPont State Forest some of what he knows about blue ghost fireflies, a tiny beetle that shows up in only a few places on the planet. Transylvania and Henderson counties are two of those places.

The rain's been coming down pretty hard. But now, after dark, it's slowed almost to a stop, and only an occasional spike of lightning brightens the clouds. Rosen has told us where to look for the fireflies, right above the ground just off the trail. If we're going to see them, it should be any time now. They're thickest between 9:30 and 10:30 p.m.

I stare. Blackness still.

Then, just about the time that I start to feel a little dizzy because I can't see the ground or trees or sky or anything that would tell me up from down, I see one. It is tiny, and I wonder if it's my imagination. Then I hear: "I see one!"

The glow hovers about three feet away at ankle height. Unlike the fireflies we chase in our front yards, this one stays lit for several seconds, sometimes as long as a minute. It doesn't twinkle so much as streak. And although the blue ghost — named for its bluish cast — is the size of a piece of rice, its light illuminates brush and trees and helps me reconnect with the solid world around me. Soon, several float among the leaves.

One bounces off my poncho. I begin to understand why these little beings create such a hullabaloo among the lucky few who've seen them. They're beautiful. Cerulean halos, like a scattering of Tinker Bells, glide through the mist. Rosen describes

evenings when he's seen hundreds of them blanket a hillside or slowly dance around tree trunks.

I hope for such a show, but my count totals less than a dozen when heavier raindrops fall. The blue ghosts sputter out.

Soon, they lit up just above the grass under our feet. And the chase was on.

I FIRST CHASED FIREFLIES on Wilora Lake Road in Mecklenburg County. That was 40-some years ago, back when it was out in the country, before the city of Charlotte swallowed it, before convenience stores and shopping malls rolled over 100-acre stretches of farmland and woods, before streetlights flooded front yards.

My parents owned three and a half acres. A stand of trees sheltered the property on one side of our small house; an open field sprouted along the other. I'm not sure why, but my dad — or rather my brothers Paul and Joe — kept the field, about an acre, mowed for years. By the time

I came along, Dad decided to let it go. For most of my childhood, it remained mostly a wild patch of tall grasses growing up around blackberry brambles, a hedge of roses, and a trio of mimosas.

The fireflies — we called them lightning bugs — showed up in the field first. My sister Suzanne and I usually made our way home to our own yard by the time the first yellow twinkles caught our eyes. While playing in the weeping willow in the backyard, we saw them first over the field. Soon, they lit up just above the grass under our feet. And the chase was on.

Wait for the blink, then rush toward it. Lock in on it; follow it, hands cupped; scoop; and capture. Squint at it through your fingers. Open your hand, and watch it walk to an edge and fly away. This is how we end a summer day in the South. To wait for the sun's retreat, then to slip barefooted across dew-cooled grass in pursuit of a natural phenomenon that seems to exist for no reason other than our delight.

By the end of summer, the lightning bugs were gone. And by the time I was in middle school, so was the field by our house. My parents gave the land to my grandmother, who moved up from Florida to be

closer to my mom and built a house there. I was happy to have her nearby, but, man, I hated to see that field go.

But things change. The city had started creeping in, widening roads and putting up lights. A mall paved over the wooded acres. The glow of a lightning bug got harder to see.

FIRST DESCRIBED in scientific literature in 1825, the blue ghost — *Phausus reticulata* — shows up in several Southern states: Georgia, South Carolina, Tennessee, as far west as Arkansas. But Rosen, who in 2010 coauthored the first published paper on the insect in more than 40 years, says the blue ghost shows up in large numbers in the Appalachian Mountains, especially in DuPont State Forest. Here, he says, they find what they need: an undisturbed site with a cool, moist, shady environment and ample water.

The forest, located between Hendersonville and Brevard, is 10,400 acres of blue ghost habitat. On most of the land, hardwoods shade thick underbrush. Lake Julia sparkles down in a valley, and the Little and Grassy rivers course across the land and over eight waterfalls.

Before it was a state forest, most of the land belonged to DuPont Industries, which, in 1957, built a huge plant here that produced high-purity silicon for the electronics industry. Later, the plant manufactured medical X-ray film. During its ownership, DuPont maintained the forest as a recreational site for its employees and people in the community.

But by 2002, the plant was closed and disassembled and hauled off the property. Not long afterward, a developer bought a large tract of the land.

Then residents learned that the forest they had retreated to for decades was about to be turned into a gated community. Nineteen of those residents decided that couldn't happen and formed The Friends of the Falls.

"We banded together and staged a PR campaign," says Aleen Steinberg, one of the original Friends and the leader of my blue ghost tour. "We got civic groups involved; the Audubon Society; and scouts, hunters, and fishermen. We sent more than 4,000 emails and letters to the governor's office."

Ultimately, the state condemned the land and settled with the devel-

oper to purchase his original tract.

"Our rallying cry was 'Save it for the people, not the privileged few,'" Steinberg says. "I put my heart and soul into saving this land."

For nearly 50 years, Steinberg has been trekking across it. She and her family discovered the forest while on

The female is earthbound. She lights up, presumably so the males can locate her. But even with a glowing abdomen, she's hard to find.

vacation in 1963. Its beauty enchanted Steinberg and her husband so much that they bought a second home here. Steinberg moved from Florida 13 years ago and today spends much of her time in the forest. Volunteering with The Friends of DuPont Forest, which evolved from The Friends of the Falls, she maintains trails; leads hikes; staffs the visitors center; and each spring, guides two or three blue ghost tours into the woods.

Her voice catches when she talks about the importance of this place.

"As long as I have breath, I'm going to work so people can get in there," she says. "I want to be able to walk past all the gates and go into heritage lands that hold endangered species and to know they're going to be there for generations to come.

"It isn't just botanists who go in there and run their hands over that lichen that they know is going to be there. It's all of us. It belongs to the people … and I'll do what I can to protect it. If it's standing in the rain looking for blue ghosts, so be it."

EVEN IN THIS PRISTINE environment, you find only pockets of blue ghosts. The tour took us not quite a mile up a gravel road and about 200 yards down a trail.

This lightning bug is fragile, Rosen tells us. It lives in the spongy leaf litter on the forest floor. If that litter gets too dry, they die. The female is earthbound. She lights up, presumably so the males can locate her. But even with a glowing abdomen, she's hard to find. In his years of pursuing the blue ghost in four states, Rosen has observed thousands of males; he's seen maybe 30 females. If their habitat is disturbed, it can take years for the population to recover.

Steinberg is disappointed by tonight's weak showing. She wants the visitors to experience the magic of a blue ghost firefly display. She's witnessed it more times than she can count, and she still gets excited at the sight of a handful of them. But she also knows that any fans she wins over will join those of us who believe we'll always need woods.

Steinberg plans on bringing out one more group. That's one more tour than she had scheduled. But tonight's turnout — in terms of people and beetles — won't do. Twenty-five people signed up, but the rain and lightning kept away all but a hardy few.

Blue ghosts don't hang around for long. They flicker through DuPont State Forest for only about four weeks, starting in May. By mid-June, they're hard to find. So Steinberg crosses her fingers and makes plans for one more trek into the woods, one more chance to marvel at a simple, fleeting wonder.

to order more

If you've enjoyed *What Makes Us Southern*, think of all your family, friends, and coworkers who would enjoy it, too!

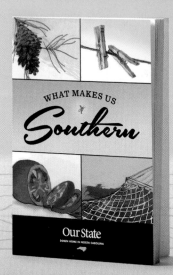

CALL THE OUR STATE STORE
— AT —
(800) 948-1409
— OR VISIT —
OURSTATESTORE.COM

Our State
DOWN HOME IN NORTH CAROLINA